PRAISE FOR THE
NEIL LABU

REASONS TO BE PRETTY

"What makes this play resonate is less its Big Theme—beauty (or lack thereof) and its discontents—than how that theme illuminates the insecurities of people who don't feel they have much to offer the world." —**BEN BRANTLEY**, *The New York Times*

"LaBute's most adult story—or at least, his most touching tale—primarily because its struggling hero, if you can call him that, really does want to grow up."

—**MICHAEL KUCHWARA**, *San Francisco Chronicle*

"The play raises provocative ideas about beauty—the significance it holds and the anxieties it creates. Even more fascinating is the underlying theme LaBute has explored ever since his breakthrough work, *In the Company of Men*—when men get together, the result is toxic."

—**JOHN DZIEMIANOWICZ**, *New York Daily News*

IN A DARK DARK HOUSE

"Refreshingly reminds us . . . that [LaBute's] talents go beyond glibly vicious storytelling and extend into thoughtful analyses of a world rotten with original sin."—**BEN BRANTLEY**, *The New York Times*

"LaBute takes us to shadowy places we don't like to talk about, sometimes even to think about . . . In the riveting *Dark House*, [he] spins a tight story practically shrink-wrapped in tension."

—ERIN MCCLAM, Newsday

"A quieter, darker, more contemplative and seemingly more personal piece of work . . . When they write the book on LaBute's career, I suspect this one will reveal more about this fascinating writer than any other of his plays."

—CHRIS JONES, Chicago Tribune

WRECKS AND OTHER PLAYS

"Superb and subversive . . . A masterly attempt to shed light on the ways in which we manufacture our own darkness. It offers us the kind of illumination that Tom Stoppard has called 'what's left of God's purpose when you take away God.'"

—JOHN LAHR, The New Yorker

"*Wrecks* is bound to be identified by its shock value. But it must also be cherished for the moment-by-moment pleasure of its masterly portraiture. There is not an extraneous syllable in LaBute's enormously moving love story." —LINDA WINER, Newsday

"Mr. LaBute here uses prototypes from Greek myths as the basis for his central story, finding Olympian extremes of behavior amid lives that seem as unthreateningly ordinary as those of your friends and neighbors (to borrow the title of a LaBute film) . . . [However,] the literary precedents that come most pointedly to mind aren't Sophocles and Euripides but

W. Somerset Maugham and O. Henry, old-fashioned writers of riddles of short stories in which pieces gradually click into a completed picture that whispers, 'Gotcha!'"

—BEN BRANTLEY, *The New York Times*

THIS IS HOW IT GOES

"LaBute's . . . most sophisticatedly structured and emotionally complex story yet, this taut firecracker of a play about an interracial love triangle may do for liberal racism what David Mamet's *Oleanna* did for sexual harassment."

—JASON ZINOMAN, *Time Out New York*

"This prolific playwright . . . has topped even his own scary self in this unrelentingly perilous, disgracefully likeable 90-minute marvel about race, romance and our inability to know everything about just about anything . . . The only unambiguous thing about this astonishing play is its quality." —LINDA WINER, *Newsday*

"The most frank, fearless look into race relations from a white dramatist since Rebecca Gilman's *Spinning into Butter.*"

—ELYSA GARDNER, *USA Today*

FAT PIG

"The most legitimately provocative and polarizing playwright at work today." —DAVID AMSDEN, *New York*

"The most emotionally engaging and unsettling of Mr. LaBute's plays since *Bash* . . . A serious step forward for a playwright who has always been most comfortable with judgmental distance." —BEN BRANTLEY, *The New York Times*

"One of Neil LaBute's subtler efforts. [It] demonstrates warmth and compassion for its characters missing in many of LaBute's previous works [and] balances black humor and social commentary in a . . . beautifully written, hilarious dissection of how societal pressures affect relationships [that] is astute and up-to-the-minute relevant." —FRANK SCHECK, *New York Post*

THE SHAPE OF THINGS

"LaBute is the first dramatist since David Mamet and Sam Shepard—since Edward Albee, actually—to mix sympathy and savagery, pathos and power . . . *The Shape of Things* . . . continues his obsession with the power games men and women play." —DONALD LYONS, *New York Post*

"LaBute . . . continues to probe the fascinating dark side of individualism . . . [His] great gift is to live in and to chronicle that murky area of not-knowing, which mankind spends much of its waking life denying." —JOHN LAHR, *The New Yorker*

"*Shape* . . . is LaBute's thesis on extreme feminine wiles, as well as a disquisition on how far an artist . . . can go in the name of art . . . Like a chiropractor for the soul, LaBute is looking for realignment, listening for the crack." —JOHN ISTEL, *Elle*

NEIL LaBUTE

THE BREAK OF NOON

NEIL LaBUTE is a critically acclaimed playwright, filmmaker, and fiction writer. His controversial works include the plays *Filthy Talk for Troubled Times, bash: latterday plays, The Distance from Here, The Mercy Seat, Fat Pig* (winner of the Outer Critics Circle Award for Outstanding Off-Broadway Play, Olivier nominee for Best Comedy), *Autobahn, This Is How It Goes, Some Girl(s), Wrecks and Other Plays, In a Dark Dark House,* and *Reasons to Be Pretty* (Tony nominee for Best Play); the films *In the Company of Men, Your Friends and Neighbors, Nurse Betty, Possession, The Wicker Man, Lakeview Terrace,* and *Death at a Funeral*; the play and film adaptation of *The Shape of Things;* and the short-story collection *Seconds of Pleasure.*

ALSO BY NEIL LABUTE

AVAILABLE FROM SOFT SKULL PRESS

Filthy Talk for Troubled Times

THE
BREAK
OF
NOON

THE BREAK OF NOON

NEIL LaBUTE

SOFT SKULL PRESS | NEW YORK

Library of Congress Cataloging-in-Publication Data

LaBute, Neil.
    The break of noon : a play / Neil LaBute.
        p. cm.
    ISBN-13: 978-1-59376-285-8 (alk. paper)
    ISBN-10: 1-59376-285-2 (alk. paper)
    1. Businessmen—Drama. 2. Vision—Religious aspects—Drama. 3. Spirituality—Drama. I. Title.
    PS3612.A28B74 2010
    812'.6—dc22

                                                                    2010013398

Cover design by Charlotte Strick
Interior design by Gretchen Achilles
Printed in the United States of America

Soft Skull Press
An Imprint of Counterpoint LLC
1919 Fifth Street
Berkeley, CA 94710

www.softskull.com
www.counterpointpress.com

Distributed by Publishers Group West

10 9 8 7 6 5 4 3 2 1

For Blaise Pascal and Howard Brenton

"Believe those who seek the truth, doubt those who find it."

ANDRÉ GIDE

"All great truths begin as blasphemies."

GEORGE BERNARD SHAW

"Jesus doesn't want me for a sunbeam."

THE VASELINES

PREFACE

I don't know what to believe.

It's not just religion I'm thinking of as I write this but a little bit of everything. I'm at some kind of crossroads, it seems, and it makes me more than a little introspective. I feel young enough but there's no way around the fact that I'm middle-aged or even a little more than that—frankly, there's no chance I'm going to make it to a hundred. I will not be one of the lucky few who end up on a Smucker's jam jar on the *Today* show during the weather report. Therefore, life as I know it is at least halfway over and that makes me wonder sometimes what I've learned or, more importantly, what I believe in anymore.

When I was young I took comfort in a youth group that I was a part of through the local non-denominational church. I learned a fair amount about the old and new testaments—I think I had a testimony of some kind and at least thought Jesus was a fine fellow, whether I was sure he was the savior of all mankind or not—but mostly I ran with the group because of a solid program of camping and hiking and other worldly pursuits. They were a fun bunch. Over the course of my youth, however, I know that I was instilled with a certain moral sense, a code of right and wrong, and a healthy interest in sin—not in committing it, necessarily, but the very idea of it—that has lasted to this day. I suppose that's why so many of my characters do bad things to one another; the author behind them is dedicated to studying the limits of this behavior and what makes it happen, why we choose good or evil and whether it really matters if no one but ourselves knows we've done it.

I suppose it's all well and good to imagine these things—as a storyteller it's my job to take my readers or my audience on the most enthralling ride possible—but what about the cost? Is it my responsibility as a writer and as a member of society to let this behavior stand or should a sin be weighed and paid for, each wrong turned to right and every story ended with "and they lived happily ever after?" Obviously, the answer from my point of view is "no." A resounding "no," in fact, and one that I think would be the same for many people if they thought about it for any length of time. There is great pleasure in the surprise ending, the unexpected turn of events, the untimely death of a character. We are taught at an early age to expect things to be a certain, soothing way in our storybooks and even in our lives—by the time we are adults we fully realize that life is a tricky little mother and that the only thing we can fully expect is the unexpected. This results in some folks not wanting that same kind of tomfoolery happening in their paid entertainment. I've met more than one person in my professional lifetime who loathed the idea of reading subtitles, looking at black and white film or following a storyline that is tricky to follow or too sad or that ends in a strange or surprising way. To these folks, entertainment means something that is easy and that they can trust. Enjoyment comes from predictability. Gladly, that is not my business—and one of many reasons that I've never been successful enough to be asked to write a sequel to anything— as I'm far more interested in being true to my characters and how their stories should end than I am to my own audiences and their collective feelings. A film or play will end as abruptly and tragically or happily as it should and not before then. I am a slave to my characters and to no one else—even as a student I hated the teacher who tried to tell me how he or she would write my play; this is teaching of the worst and most hollow kind. Of course that teacher would do things differently; he or she was a different person with a different perspective. The only thing that matters when I'm writing is how *I* want to write the story, and that's what I try to stay true to, whether as a writer, a teacher, or a viewer. As an observer you are free to judge the results.

The only people who shouldn't be judging anything, in fact, are the writer, the director, and their cast. Leave it up to the paying audience to decide if the play is good or the lead character is likable. Can your Nazi wife-beater protagonist ever be seen as a sympathetic character? Is he a good or bad person? I'm the last person to ask. I'm the writer; I just tell it like I see it. What I do still have faith in is the power of the stage and the belief that *interesting* is more important in writing than *good* or *bad*. Give me a character that makes me want to know what happens next any day over the tiresome and toothsome conventional hero or heroine. I have little—no, make that no—faith in conventions.

So yes, I struggle with faith and therefore it is inevitable that it would make its way to the page. The story of a man who tries to be good but is held back by his former life seemed like an intriguing idea to me. To spend some time with a person who is honestly striving to be a better person in a world that could care less helped me wrestle with these questions once again in my own life. I still believe Jesus to be a good man. I'm still quite sure I won't make it to a hundred. I am absolutely certain I'm a better and braver artist than I am a person.

Such is life. On we go. Anything forward (and sometimes even backward) is progress.

NEIL LaBUTE

THE BREAK OF NOON

PRODUCTION HISTORY

The Break of Noon had its world premiere on October 28, 2010 at the Lucille Lortel Theatre in New York City, in a production by the Manhattan Class Company (MCC). Director: Jo Bonney. Artistic Directors: Bernie Telsey and Robert LuPone. Associate Artistic Director: Will Cantler. Scenic designer: Neil Patel. Lighting: David Weiner. Sound designer: Darron West. Costume designer: Emilio Sosa. Production manager: BD White. Stage manager: Christina Lowe.

MAN / JOHN   David Duchovny

At the time this edition went to press, the remainder of the roles had not yet been cast.

CHARACTERS

MAN / JOHN	male, middle-aged
LAWYER	male, fifties
HOST	female, thirties
GINGER	female, middle-aged
DIVA MIDNIGHT	female, twenties
DETECTIVE	male, forties
JESSIE	female, middle-aged

SETTING

Various places in and around a big city.

TIME

Present.

NOTES

A slash denotes an attempt at interruption between the present line and the next speakers line.

The text that follows represents the script as the production went into rehearsals for the New York premiere.

Silence. Darkness.

*A light snaps on. Harsh. Direct. It reveals a man seated on a metal
chair in front of us. He shields his eyes.*

MAN   (*hesitating*) . . . I'm . . . my name is—sorry, that light is
    really strong and it's *shining right into my . . . could you . . .
    maybe . . . ?*

*The light is adjusted. By degrees. Finally the MAN smiles and nods
that he can continue.*

MAN   Thanks a lot. Thank you for . . . it's much better that way.
    I don't know what it was before but it caught me square in
    the—it doesn't matter. That's great. (*Beat.*) So, from the
    beginning of my—how it started? Right? Yeah. From the . . .

*He takes a deep breath, nodding. Starts to speak. Stops. Another
breath or two before he can begin.*

MAN   . . . it was almost twelve. I remember that because I've
    noticed—I mean, from where my office is—that just before,
    like, a minute or two at most . . . when the clock's just getting
    ready to strike, you know it's time because lots of people get
    up early and grab their stuff so that they can be out the door
    first. Or, well, on the first *elevator*, I'm saying. On their way
    down just as the hour hits. People do that all the time. Yep.
    (*Beat.*) So I knew it—I could already tell what time it was but I
    wasn't in any kind of hurry. No. I figured that I might go down
    and get something, a sandwich or whatever, but there wasn't

any rush. Let the crowd go by and then I'd head on down, that's the way I usually go about it on a day when I don't have a lunch set up or that kinda deal . . . I'm pretty basic. My needs and all that. I'm good-to-go with a half sandwich and a soup or even, like, the special they've got at the corner deli. I'm happy to live with that—sausage and peppers or whatever they're serving. The *gyro* platter, even. That's fine. By now, I'm a pro at lunch.

He smiles and stops for a minute, looking out into the darkness. He squints, then continues.

MAN   Anyhow, that's what I did. I did that . . . let my colleagues stampede each other and then I started to get up, went to use the restroom and finally headed downstairs. (*Beat.*) The shot that I heard—of course in the beginning I didn't know what it was but, yeah, now I know it was a gun—came when I was washing my hands. I was doing that, *drying* them, actually, and I heard this "pop" sound from somewhere in the building. Now, you have to understand what I'm describing for you here is only a sense of the place. It's huge. Sanford-Gross? Place is massive . . . so, when I say folks are heading out and I'm doing this and that . . . it's still almost completely full of people. Lots and lots of my, you know, coworkers are about to have their lunch. It's a bit of a madhouse in there. (*Beat.*) It honestly is.

He takes a breath. Almost a sigh.

MAN   So, my thinking here is, and I'm just . . . this is
only speculation because I know they still have a lot of
whaddayacallit to do? *Forensic* work and all that, but I figure
he came up on that noon elevator. Right? Now that sounds—
there's no such thing as a "noon" elevator, those things are
up and down all day long, opening and closing all the time,
but I'm saying that he must've planned it that way. Being on
the one that arrived right when they're all waiting there to
jump on for an hour break. Doesn't that seem . . . ? (*Beat.*)
Maybe not, maybe it's just a pure coincidence, but it does
seem kinda logical to me . . . I mean, look, the guy knows
the layout, has a sense of the routine, I'm saying of the
overall office routine, and therefore he shows up right at the
busiest time of the day. I mean, arguably. Mornings are very
frenzied around there, too, but the evenings are generally
less so—with lots of folks out for drinks or headed off to the
suburbs after their last meeting out of the office, that sort of
thing. Don't like to think about it, you know, as if *I* was him—
that's creepy—but it's true. If you wanted to make the kind
of, like, statement that he did, create panic and widespread
havoc on a major scale, then you'd pretty much do what it
seems like he did. You'd come into the place with your guns
blazing as all these men and women are wandering around
taking drink orders or grabbing their coats and not a thought
in their heads other than a Cobb salad or maybe the *shrimp
basket* over at that Irish pub thing that's catty-corner from
us on Sixth. (*Beat.*) *That's* how you create chaos in about
two seconds flat. And I do think that's what he did. From the
looks of it. (*Beat.*) Like I said, I wasn't down near that end of
the hall when he first came in, but those sounds that I heard,

followed by all the screaming that came right afterwards—
well, it must've been something very much like that. (*Sits up.*)
I don't suppose anybody from that general area made it out
of—no, 'course not . . . from what your people've told me. I
know the shots started happening more quickly after the first
one—the noise his thing was making, that rifle—it was like
one of those, what, some kind of machine gun, right? Some
of the police guys who got to me said that. He was using an
automatic weapon—that's what they said. An "AK–47" or
whatever those things are known as . . . Russian? Right? It's
a gun from Europe or something. And that is what he's using
as he wanders through the place. Plus handguns and some
knives, even. Someone said he stabbed a few—one of my
assistants, this nice girl from Florida, only moved up here
about *eight* months ago with her two kids. He, ahhhhh . . .
guess he cut her throat in the copy room. Where he found her
down on the floor. Trying to pretend she was dead. (*Laughs.*)
Why would she do that? I mean, I guess you do all kinda
shit when your life's . . . and she was just guessing. Right?
I mean, with all that's going on . . . she doesn't know how
many guys are doing this, if it's, like, a *gang* or something. So
she goes down on the tile there, see, so she can pretend like
she's already been shot or whatnot, I mean, I might've done
the very same thing. Yeah. Really. Problem is—thing she
couldn't know—there's only one man. He comes to the Xerox
area there, sees her playing possum and knows *he* didn't kill
her . . . and then stops, in the middle of this, you know, his
rampage, to do that. To her. That's what he did. He goes and
he slits her throat and then he—he took the time to do that.

Yeah. (*Beat.*) I'm sorry but that is just sorta off-the-goddamn-charts from what I know about human behavior. It really is.

The MAN *stops for a moment, fighting back tears. He turns away and then looks back. Shaking his head.*

MAN   That's the kinda stuff you read on, like, the Internet—not *live* through, lunchtime of some regular workday in September. It just isn't. And I don't know how to come back from that, how you put things in any kind of perspective after you have that happen to you. I mean, luckily for me I had this whole, you know . . . thing happen, and I *still* have nightmares about it! I can put it all into some . . . tangible Christian context but I just know that that's not going to stop me from being doubled over by guilt and fear and, and flashbacks that're all—it's hard for me to imagine a time when I'll be okay with this. When I'll be back to being that guy again. "Me." So . . . it's . . .

He squints again, holding a hand up toward the lights. Waits.

MAN   I'm sorry? (*Beat.*) Oh, sure, absolutely—so there were those first moments, this beat of just pure . . . panic inside me. One *moment* where I'm thinking—because now I get it—I can feel what's going on and I wanna tell you, it's not like a movie. It is not. Like, when you're a kid and you see something on TV or at the drive-in and think, "I could get out of that! I'd find a way through the fire or the, like, *natives* or Nazis or whatever." Bunch of bank robbers. But you don't.

Most people get shot or crushed by concrete or have a heart attack or something. Very few of us turn out to be heroes. It's just not the way this stuff works out. But we always *think* we're immortal—we feel like we're the one who's not gonna die, who'll stop where they are and never grow old. We do, though. We do age and get sick or ripped apart by *sharks* or end up on that wrong plane or, or, or on the Israeli *Olympic* team . . . we make these choices that seem like nothing at the time, so frivolous and happenstance and then, just like . . . (*snaps his fingers*) that! You're a story on ABC for ten minutes and you were dead wrong—you're just a person and life's over and that was that. Your one chance is gone. (*Beat.*) That's how *I* felt. Right then. My life was . . . I . . . I'm sorry.

He takes a moment to gather his thoughts. Not wanting to go back to that place.

MAN   . . . this is hard. It's really . . . just . . . yeah. Hard. (*Beat.*) I knew that's how I was gonna end up—some *statistic*—if I didn't do something. Make a move or get myself outta there. Hide. And so I did. Yeah. I scrambled outta the bathroom and kept my head down, moving off between the first set of those—what're they called?—the room dividers that I came to down the corridor. Heading the other way. I kept down low and darted back toward the rear of our floor, figuring I could make it to an exit or something, use the stairs, before I'd be spotted. There's this eerie sort of silence in the air now—I suppose the initial panic had subsided, that moment where everybody first saw the guy and he opened fire. There was a lot of yelling and, like, the screams of women then, but as he moved past and that first bunch was killed—after that moment, I think we were all just trying to survive from then on. Find some corner to crawl into, get out a door or some side window, *anything*. See, we're too high up to jump, really—it's six floors down—but if you are trapped like that you'll do whatever to try and live, it's true . . . leap, even. Leap onto rocks or into some burning pit of, like, *cobras* . . . because we think there might be a chance! There is a *chance* I'll survive and it's better than being shot down by some crazy person in my business suit. Coffee cup in my hand . . . (*Beat.*) So there I go—I'm crawling, all down on my hands and knees practically, trying to figure out which side of the room he's headed to or which one of the aisles he's gonna come down, or might use next. As I move, I'm passing these open portals into other people's offices . . . you know, like, all the mini-offices for the salespeople and junior execs who sit right out in the middle of the floor with their little . . . plants and crap, pictures of their kids out for all of us to see—and then, every so often. BAM! BAM-BAM! That sound of his gun. Firing. You know? BAM! It was . . . BAM! You know? (*Beat.*) God . . .

The MAN *rubs a hand across his face, trying to wipe away some of the memories.*

MAN   I see folks I haven't talked to in *weeks*—you work in the same company but you just don't have time to stand around and be so funny with everyone you meet, know what I mean? These are a bunch of people that're my colleagues but I'm not out at the bar with 'em, night after night. I can't even remember some of their first names! But I see them there, a few of 'em, anyway, as I'm sneaking along. Grown men, hunched up under their desks and weeping into their cell phones, calling the police or their wives—*anybody*—trying to figure out what to do next. How to . . . or dead. Most of 'em were already dead . . . it was terrible. And horrible. And just what you'd imagine it would be like. It wasn't like the movies, I know I've told you that, but that's the only frame of reference I have for it and it just wasn't that . . . I didn't feel all strong or smart or like I could move any mountains. I pissed my pants, that's what *I* did. I saw Marjorie, one of the, ahhh, older ladies from Word Processing over on the floor— she'd been hit somewhere in the back or something, I'm not sure—and she had pulled herself down the hall towards the break room. I don't think she ever even saw what hit her. I really don't. Blood pouring down the back of her blouse and, and some other guy, this salesman who . . . he stops in about once a *month*—Yeah! How's that for luck?—with most of his face blown off. He had to've gotten shot right up front, early on because those guys hardly even check in with reception and they're out the door—how he got here, down so far toward the rear exits, I dunno . . . I don't think he could've run back, not with his face like that, but you really would be amazed what the human body is capable of when the adrenaline kicks in and your will to live takes over. So I guess he might've just took off running once he got hit. Anyway, he was dead, too. (*Beat.*) And then I saw him. The gunman. He turned this corner about fifty yards down the hall from me and looked both ways. That's when I—and I don't know why, I really don't, but I—that's when I snapped the photograph. Of him. Right then. I guess the flash was—he spotted me down on the floor there and fired off a few rounds. That's how I got this . . . (*Points to his leg.*) One of those bullets kicked up off the linoleum and grazed my leg—it's alright now, they treated me right afterwards, but that's how it happened. Even though I was hit I got up and ran off, down this short passage to the other side of the room. I could hear his boots—he was wearing some sort of outfit when they found him, right? And I could hear that, the heavy sound of his boots on the floor. As he's running toward me. I was frantic now, thinking as I'm going, "He's seen me! He's *seen* me!!" And not knowing what to do. I can hear—it's almost, like, surrealistic by this time—helicopters outside and that sound of the police talking over their big—not megaphones, not those, cheerleaders use those . . . but bullhorns. Yeah. Those. You guys're outside the place and I can see the smoke rising up from tear gas—the color it's making with the light as it comes in the windows on that side of the office, it's almost beautiful—and now is the time I find myself the most scared. In those, ohh, probably only two or three minutes before I'm found, see, because this is the bit where you *so* want to live—You are close! You can make it!—but this guy is coming now. He knows the authorities are on the way in and he's spotted me as another guy he can kill before it's over. I can hear the shouting of the officers as they're pouring into the room, their shadows dancing off the . . . but now I can see that I've got myself backed into a corner. After that moment when I got hit—when he took a shot at me—I got myself turned around and headed east instead of west—the exit is on the opposite side of the room! There's nothing but the water cooler and this . . . soft-seating area over in that corner of the building and it's where

I've crawled to. I bump into a love seat and I immediately realize what I've done. I realize it and I burst out crying right there. How could I be so *stupid*?! Huh? Oh-Dear-God. (*Beat.*) And then there's this—and this is the part your people didn't want to hear from me earlier but I need to say it . . . because it's how it went and if you want my statement then you'll listen to me and you will write it down. Alright? (*Waits.*) Fine. I was there, down on my hands and knees and I know this guy is gonna come around the corner any second and I am gonna be the last sonofabitch he kills before they bring him down, I just *know* it! I saw his face earlier and he's one of . . . I recognize him from the recruits that were sandwiched in late last year— he's one of our own employees, a customer service rep who sits about ten feet from my office, chatting on a headset all day to very irate customers. And I am sure that it's a shitty job and I'd hate it, too, but it is not something that would make me break with reality and go off on some shooting spree! It's not, no, but I just can't process any of that right then, I'm aware that I recognize the guy and I can feel him as he's coming around—and then it happens. I'm about to get back on my feet, make a run down the hallway back toward where I hear the police when this voice—and I am *not* talking about in my head, no, this is not *in* my head or some other employee or me being *disoriented* by the smoke and the panic and anything of that nature—I stop and hear a voice call out to me. Using my name, and it says to me, "Remain here and you will be safe, John. Stay where you are and you shall be saved." (*Beat.*) Yes. Now, you can make fun of me all you want—and I heard the word "shall" like I hear you now, so say what you want. I heard this and it was spoken directly to me. John Smith. And so that's what I did. I stayed there, I closed my eyes and I stayed down on my knees. And it's all I remember until I was . . . sitting next to an ambulance talking to you guys and having my ankle looked at. Yes. That is it. That's the truth as I'm aware of it. Alright?

The MAN *stops for a moment—he hasn't taken a breath for a bit. His shoulders rise and fall a few times. He looks around. Waiting. Looks up when he's asked a question:*

MAN   No. I . . . I have no idea about any of that. How it happened. Yeah, I know . . . *yes.* I get that. But I didn't see it go down and wasn't aware of . . . no. You found me there, still on my knees and the guy was dead—what was his name? Juan or . . . something like that. I barely knew him. I think his name's "Juan." A guy who had been laid off. (*Beat.*) . . . listen, I don't *care* if he was lying there in front of me—I don't give a damn if that's—I didn't kill him! Don't you think I'd tell you if I'd done something like that? Heroic. I'm not a . . . I took his picture, that's all I was able to . . . *that's* what I did. That one picture. But I'm no hero . . .

The MAN *looks around but there is no response in return. He continues.*

MAN   I'm telling the truth here. I was on my knees . . . down there on my knees and I'm praying and there comes a voice, this beautiful, deep, clear voice that tells me what I told you and so I did what it commanded. And here you see me, before you and alive. I know what I heard. And what I didn't.

This is a miracle—I know that is old-fashioned and people don't like to hear that stuff anymore but you call it what you want. It was not SWAT that brought me here . . . it was not my own ingenuity, I'm not some Bruce Willis who saved the day—my Heavenly Father stepped in like one of those, you know . . . like a story from the Bible where men were once placed in *ovens* or inside of caverns with lions about, like a page from Exodus or—I was saved! I was seen as, as worthy and forgiven and that is how I sit before you today. Believe me or don't. Make me some figure of ridicule if you wish. The truth is here, right *here* in front of you. God saved me. He did. For some reason on that particular day he reached a hand down and he saved me. (*Beat.*) No. Actually, *no*, he did more than that—no one else survived, not *one* other person made it out and that is—it was *me* who was chosen. I don't say it with *pride* but as a simple fact . . . God chose only me. Only *me*. Jonathan Smith. (*Beat.*) I alone was *spared*.

The MAN *puts his head down. Glances up at that light again.*

MAN   Could you . . . ? Nothing. No. It's alright. (*Beat.*) I'd like to rest now. If that's . . .

He lowers his head into his hands. Rubs his eyes. Stays with his face covered.

A burst of intense light carries us on to:

An office. JOHN *sitting with a* LAWYER—*in his fifties—at a table. He is sorting through papers and pictures. He slows down to study one as he finishes a glass of water.*

LAWYER   . . . oh. Jesus. That's . . . / Oh.

JOHN   I know. / Yes.

LAWYER   That's . . . really . . . *shit*.

JOHN   Yeah. I know.

LAWYER   . . . ahhh. Huh. (*Looks closer.*) That is a pretty clear shot of—wait, what is that? She's on the . . . *what* is that?

JOHN   It's from an angle. See? (*Turns picture.*) There.

LAWYER   Oh, right, I see, that's her . . . (*Looks.*) I still don't know what that is.

JOHN   That?

LAWYER   Yeah. Right *there*. Is that her . . . *tit*?

JOHN   Her breast. Yes. (*Points.*) It's on the—they're not connected.

LAWYER   Oh! So that's . . . I get it. That's her . . . it isn't *on* her torso. It's over in a separate sort of . . . huh. / A little pile. It got literally . . . *blown* off. Right? I mean, like . . . boom!

JOHN   Right. / That's right.

The LAWYER *looks up at* JOHN *for a moment—studies him. Silence. He goes back to the stack. Holds another up.*

LAWYER   Damn! (*Another photo.*) Who's this? Is . . . ?

He holds up a photo—almost a portrait—of a beautiful young girl. JOHN *reacts, reaching out for it.*

JOHN Sorry, no, that's—(*Explains.*) That one's my daughter. Chrissy. At a school play.

LAWYER I see. (*Beat.*) She wasn't . . . at the . . . ?

JOHN No! God, no . . . no, I just printed all of the, you know . . . everything I could pull off the phone there. The whole file. I only took the one picture during the . . .

LAWYER Got it. Alright. Wheeew!!

The LAWYER *sets this photo aside and shuffles through the rest. He finally goes back to the first photo.*

LAWYER Is that him? This guy?

JOHN Ummmm . . . yeah. He's—that's the gunman. Right there.

LAWYER God! Look at his eyes! The way the sun just caught his . . . wow!! Whole thing's just...creepy. (*Looking at John.*) I can't even *imagine* how you're . . . very brave stuff. What you did.

JOHN . . . Thank you.

LAWYER It's really just . . . well, shocking. When you think about it. And you were *right* in the . . . shit! It's frightening.

JOHN Yes. (*Beat.*) But I had the Lord on my side during it all.

LAWYER Right.

JOHN He came into my heart during all of this and so I can . . . / I'm free to . . . be . . .

LAWYER Yeah, about that. / Listen. John. We need to talk about this. *Now.*

JOHN Alright.

LAWYER You can't just . . . look, I know you've been through a lot—the whole psychological . . . how's that going, by the way?

JOHN . . . it's fine. *I'm* fine, I just need to . . .

LAWYER They did get you a therapist, right? Someone for you to . . . ? / Great.

JOHN . . . yes, but . . . / I'm not sure he's . . .

LAWYER That's good, no, that's terrific but you need to . . . / You really should be . . .

JOHN . . . I'm not *certain* that I can . . . / I'm . . .

LAWYER John! *Stop.* We're talking over each other here and I need you to . . . wait. Hear what I have to say first. (*Sighs.*) You cannot keep doing this. Going around with the, ummmm, "conversion" story, okay? You can't.

JOHN . . . but . . .

LAWYER *No.* You cannot. / John . . .

JOHN Yes, I can. / Because it's true.

LAWYER Know what? That's the kind of thing that could put me out of a job. The "truth" . . . (*Smiles.*) I'm not saying it didn't happen.

JOHN Good, because . . .

LAWYER I'm not gonna argue religion with you at this particular moment, alright? / And I'm someone who loves to argue . . .

JOHN That's fine, but . . . / I'll bet!

LAWYER Seriously, I do. (*Beat.*) When I was a kid, I'd take the side that nobody else wanted and I mean about anything! My mom . . . woman hated me, and I don't mean in the "Ohhhh, that boy of mine" way—I'm saying it was actual hatred. / Outright.

JOHN No. / That's not . . .

LAWYER You know her?

JOHN Of course not.

LAWYER So then please don't tell me about my mom if you don't mind—she couldn't wait for me to graduate, to get outta the house. I bet we haven't talked more than a *dozen* times or so since I was eighteen. I am now fifty-three. (*Beat.*) Bitch is alive and well down in Arizona, I pay for everything—amazing how "guilt" works!—and yet it's all done by my business guy and cashier's checks and whatnot. / It is what it is.

JOHN Jeez. / That's horrible.

LAWYER That's life. That's my life and I would not trade it with anybody—you think I envy *you*? Huh? You could be dead now . . .

JOHN That's true. But I'm not.

LAWYER Exactly! You're not, and that's your life that you're living at this moment. You've lived through the most . . . I mean, what're they saying on the TV? It's one if not *the* worst office shooting in history. In American *history* and you were right there in the middle of it! Taking a *picture*! It blows my mind, it really does.

JOHN I know. (*Nods.*) Listen, I'm aware of just how blessed I am—people think it's luck but it's not, that's what I need to make clear to everyone—that's why I'm . . .

LAWYER *No.* Don't say it. Not the "God" thing.

The LAWYER *gets up and crosses to pour himself a glass of water. Offers to* JOHN, *who declines.*

JOHN No thank you.

LAWYER Sure? (*Waits.*) Six glasses a day of this crap, my doctor insists.

JOHN I've heard that. It's supposed to . . .

LAWYER Yeah, for ladies who want to look *twenty* again! For people who go to "Curves" and buy into that "Weight Watchers" bullshit. Not some old guy like me who just wants to work and eat and take a nice, gracious dump a few times a week. I need to drink water like I'm some refugee kid in *Asia*? (*Shakes his head.*) I don't think so! Hell, I don't even like *kids*, but hey . . .

JOHN . . . I don't know . . .

LAWYER Exactly! Nobody knows anything—not that it stops this guy from speaking his mind, and *me* paying the jerk for the pleasure. Ahh, well. (*Drains the glass.*) That's two.

He puts the glass down and turns back to JOHN. Lays his hands on top of JOHN's shoulders.

LAWYER You need to listen to me now, and then I will shut up. / I promise.

JOHN Alright. / Okay.

LAWYER You like religion? You think you've heard the voice of God? Fine. You keep this up: people-will-crucify-you. There, that's a religious word for you and I'm not even speaking metaphorically. This *cannot* be the way you go about discussing the . . .

JOHN No, I have to . . . *no*. God told me to . . .

LAWYER Stop! It's my turn to talk, remember? So you listen. You hired me, you bring all this . . . *stuff* . . . to me, ask my opinion . . . *pay* me to give you my learned . . . so hear me out. (*Picks up the photo.*) John. John Smith. How much do you make a year?

JOHN What're you . . . ?/ That's not your . . .

LAWYER Your salary. / What is it? (*Beat.*) I'm your *lawyer*, John, I'm not going to judge you.

JOHN I'm . . . it's roughly $100,000 annually. / And there are bonuses, too, if I'm . . .

LAWYER Okay, that's . . . / Listen, that's fine. One-hundred thou. Very respectable. And you probably have a 401K and some . . . whatever. You're tucking a little bit away for the future. You've gotta be, what? How old? Hmmm?

JOHN I'm forty-five. (*Beat.*) My hair is . . .it's all . . .

LAWYER Forty-five years old. Right? (*Holds up the photo.*) This picture you took—a photo that you got on your cell during what is now being regularly described as a "massacre . . . "

JOHN Yes?

LAWYER Consider it El Dorado. Or Fort Knox. A leisurely dip in the goddamn fountain of youth. (*Beat.*) I can get you three million for it. Today. Probably more.

JOHN For that picture?

LAWYER For this *very* snapshot. *People* magazine or the *Enquirer—The New York Times,* even . . . you think they're above this? No way in hell they are! You see any of the London bombing photos a few years back? This is a *hundred* times better! You got *bodies.* Better yet, you've got body *parts!* (*Beat.*) Whomever you give this to as an exclusive, with your story—and I'm not even figuring international rights into that—you're about to become a goddamn phenomenon.

JOHN I see. (*Beat.*) That's not why I came to you . . . / Not for any . . . sort of . . .

JOHN *doesn't know what to say. His* LAWYER *nods at this.*

LAWYER John, I even believe that. I do. / But the fact remains . . .

JOHN It's the truth. I was *told* to . . . by . . .

LAWYER See there? Right there. / That.

JOHN What? / *What*?

LAWYER The "voice" shit again and you're—that stops now or you're fucked. I don't like to use that kind of language when I'm in the office but you need to hear it. Okay? There's one way for you to bring this all down like a house of goddamn cards! (*Beat.*) You keep on with the "God spoke to me" crap and you *might* get a couple bucks from Pat Robertson and a seat on the *700 Club* for a few weeks. / Am I making myself clear here?

JOHN I see. / Yes.

LAWYER It's cynical, I know. And yet there it is. The truth.

JOHN If that's . . . I'm not sure that I can . . .

LAWYER John, I'm just here to assess all this and to give you my advice. You're paying for me to do that. I can do nothing less.

He stands, pours himself another glass of water. Drinks.

LAWYER Ugh. God. (*Shivers.*) That's three.

JOHN I understand that you're just giving me a glimpse of what you . . . feel is . . .

LAWYER No, John, in this case I'm giving you the facts. There's only *one* here, in fact, and I'm here to give it to you. "Fact."

JOHN I don't understand.

LAWYER   You're sitting on top of a diamond mine. That little SIM card of yours is a mint—but you cannot keep talking about God! So you're gonna have to choose.

JOHN   That's . . . no, I won't go against what I've been commanded to do. / I can't! The very fact that I'm . . . the whole *purpose* of my escaping there was to, you know . . . to . . .

LAWYER   John . . . / *Please* hear what I'm . . .

JOHN   *No.* Give it away—I didn't shoot it for money. It wasn't a calculated . . . this was a record. My *testament* . . . I thought I was going to *die* and I'm not going to . . . no! That's my answer. Do as you see fit—if they pay you then give most of it away to charity. Half.

LAWYER   Yeah? And the other half? Because people will be . . . you know. Curious.

JOHN   My wife. Or . . . you know. Ex-wife. I should leave a portion for her, although I need to speak with her, too. There's still a few things that we're . . . and my daughter. That's . . . any that would go to *me* I would like to give away. / At some point . . .

LAWYER   I can do that. / Fine. You think about it.

JOHN   And you'll tell them the story?

LAWYER   If you make me. At gunpoint. / *Joking* . . .

JOHN   Please. / That's not very . . . funny . . .

LAWYER   Then "yes," I will. I can't promise you what we'll get for it—I *can* promise you it's gonna be a lot less with the Jesus bit left in.

JOHN   It wasn't Jesus. / I don't *think* it was . . .

LAWYER   Save it. / I'm not interested in the—I'll see what I can do. (*Picks up the picture again.*) So that's the *guy*. The shooter.

JOHN   Who? Oh. Yes. That's him.

LAWYER   With the . . . ?

JOHN   Lemme see . . . yes. (*Pointing.*) Right there. You can see that he's . . . with his mouth open and he's . . .

LAWYER   Smiling. Shit! He was right . . . *you* took that of him? / While he was, I mean . . . ?

JOHN   Yes. / I just snapped it.

LAWYER   What're you, like, Robert Capa?

JOHN   I don't know who that is . . .

LAWYER   He was a guy who used to take war—that's not important. What he did was dangerous.

JOHN   Oh.

LAWYER   *How* the fuck did you get that?

JOHN   He was turned slightly. He didn't see me.

LAWYER   And you . . . ? / I mean this is worth, probably . . . *lots*. Wow. Goddamn.

JOHN   Yes. / Please don't keep . . . the profanity.

LAWYER   Sorry. (*Looks at photo.*) People are gonna *freak* when they see this—and some might even hate you for it, so . . . be prepared.

JOHN   Yeah. I suppose so.

LAWYER   And the cops are . . . what? I mean . . .

JOHN   They confiscated my phone for evidence but the photo is mine. They kept one for their records. / But they can't stop me showing it or . . . you know . . .

LAWYER   Fine. / Good. Nice. (*Looks again.*) What is he, some, Mexican or something? / Didn't I read he was a Mexican guy, or . . . ?

JOHN I'm not sure. / I don't . . . *Honduran*, maybe. I think it's Honduras . . . or, or . . .

LAWYER *Whatever.* He's from someplace else—our Mr. *Diaz.* It's a good angle. Fine. / We can use that. The "foreign" element.

JOHN What is? / Oh. (*Beat.*) How?

LAWYER He's not one of us—it's a nice selling point. (*Smiles.*) John! Try and be happy! Relax, go get a *massage*, for Christ's sake. Somebody's about to become very, very rich. . .

The LAWYER *pats* JOHN *heavily on the shoulder and heads back to the water. Pours another glass. Downs it.*

LAWYER . . . shit. (*Makes a face.*) That's four.

A burst of intense light carries us on to:

A forest. Out near the water. Sound of a summer day that might lull you to sleep. Perfect.

JOHN carries a basket and a blanket, with a lovely woman on his arm. Ex-wife, in fact—GINGER SMITH. Almost his age. She has her eyes covered by a scarf and is being guided along by her former spouse.

JOHN   . . . follow me.

GINGER   This is silly . . .

JOHN   Just a bit farther.

GINGER   John, really, come on. The ground is—I can still walk! I'm not *that* old . . .

JOHN   Ginger, please, it's fun! Lemme help you, okay? / Step over the . . .

GINGER   . . . John . . . / You're making it harder . . .

JOHN   Come on . . . / We're almost there.

GINGER   For heaven's sake. / Good.

JOHN   Another ten yards or so . . . just . . .

GINGER   This is a great way to twist an ankle, you know.

JOHN   I won't let you.

GINGER   I'm serious, and then I'm . . . I've got my cycling class tomorrow and I don't wanna be all . . .

JOHN   We're here. This is it.

GINGER   Good. (*Points.*) Lemme take it off, then.

JOHN   I'll help, it's twisted . . . no, here . . .

GINGER   I'm . . . *don't* . . . my hair's getting all . . .

GINGER stops speaking when the blindfold is removed. She is a little dumbfounded, staring out at the landscape.

JOHN Well?

GINGER Ummm . . . huh. / Wow.

JOHN Isn't it great? / Right?

GINGER I'm . . . yeah, it is. It's, you know . . . nostalgic or whatever. I guess.

JOHN Gee, *thanks*. (*Beat.*) I thought it'd mean something. Does to me.

GINGER It's . . . I don't get it. John?

JOHN I brought you here. To this . . . *our* spot.

GINGER Yes. You did. Our spot from twenty years ago. (*Beat.*) So*ooo?*

JOHN Doesn't it do anything for you? I mean . . .

GINGER Sure, yeah. I'm . . . (*Beat.*) Is this part of your therapy or something? Because . . .

JOHN No, of course not! No . . . (*Laughs.*) It's nothing like that, I just thought we'd have a, you know, a moment together. Us. Away from Chrissy or lawyers or . . . that sort of thing. Like when we first got married. Here and alone and in love . . . that it might stir up something. Some *memories*. (*Beat.*) Is that crazy?

GINGER No, no, not really, it's just . . . it's a bit unexpected, that's all.

She studies him for a moment. Carefully. He looks away.

GINGER . . . the hair is . . . wow. / It's amazing.

JOHN I know. / It was literally overnight. I'm in the hospital, I go to sleep, and pow!

GINGER Ha! (*Beat.*) My God. And completely *white*? That's not you doing any . . . ?

JOHN Course not, no! Why would I? (*Beat.*) *No.*

JOHN is carrying a large bag with stuff in it. He moves to arrange things and after a beat GINGER joins him, in the groove of it. JOHN puts his coat down for her.

JOHN Gorgeous day, huh?

GINGER Uh-huh . . .

JOHN Beautiful! Look at those clouds . . .

GINGER Yeah, they're . . . yep. *Cloudy.*

JOHN No, not cloudy, but—I mean, I'm not contradicting you, but—they're . . .

GINGER I know . . . it's okay . . .

JOHN Call it "cloudy" if you want to, but it's just . . . I think it's gorgeous out here.

A smile from JOHN. GINGER tries to join in—a moment is shared between them. Not much of one, but it's something.

JOHN So. "Here we are." (*Grins.*) I just . . . I think you'll like the food I got. Some nice sandwiches and stuff. Salads.

GINGER Great . . .

JOHN That one tuna that you love, with those, ahh, what-do-you-call-'ems? / You know . . .

GINGER What? / Oh, yeah, scallions. I like that. (*Beat.*) You went to that little . . . ? Over by my cousin's? / By Jesse's apartment.

JOHN Uh-huh. / Yes. That deli over on 23rd. Not the Jewish place, the high-end one . . .

GINGER Nice. *Expensive.* (*Beat.*) And way too much! Why'd you
get so much stuff? This is . . .

JOHN Hey, only the best for us, right? / It's a new leaf for me—
being more carefree.

GINGER I guess. / I ordered pizza for Chrissy, so I'll try not to
feel, like, you know, too *gluttonous* here or anything . . .

JOHN Right! Nah, she'll be fine. / What?

GINGER *starts to open a plastic container, then stops.*

GINGER 'Spose so. / John, we need to, I mean, I wanna . . .
talk. This is, like . . . it's time. I know you're still recovering,
but . . .

JOHN Alright . . . / What do you mean?

GINGER I'm just . . . what's up?/ You're . . . come on. *This.* All
this you're doing here. It's . . . I saw you on the news and you
were *so* . . . what's the point of it? I mean . . .

JOHN It's . . . nothing. I'm spreading the word.

GINGER John. (*Beat.*) *John* . . .

JOHN . . . Ginger . . .

GINGER What? I'll eat your food, I promise . . . we'll have our
little "moment" and everything here, we will, but you need to
tell me. You *have* to. John, what's up with you lately? / Come
on . . .

JOHN Nothing. / I don't know what you mean . . .

GINGER Listen . . . if you're still feeling . . . I'm just saying that
I'd understand.

JOHN No, come on, I don't wanna turn this into one of our big
discussion times. I don't.

GINGER No, I wasn't. / I was not gonna do that.

JOHN Yes, uh-huh . . . / Yes you were . . .

GINGER No, John, I just want to . . . you're . . .

JOHN I want this to be about us right now, okay? Can it just be
that? A minute out in the country with my wife . . . away from
the . . . stuff! My God, I have people camped at my door,
every day, *photographers* and . . .

GINGER "Ex." / "Ex"-wife.

JOHN What? / Okay, right. Yes. Sure. *Whatever.* With my "ex" for
a bit . . . away from the legal questions and family therapies,
nights out with our daughter so she feels involved and loved.
Look, I'm just trying to do something for you and me. Okay?
The original *couple* in all this, you know? I mean . . . hell . . .

GINGER I get that, I see it now, and that's nice of you . . . it
is. John, I was just asking a question, putting it out there,
because you seem different to me. Acting a bit differently,
so I said something . . . if that's not the case, then I'm sorry.
(*Beat.*) I know that you've got people *hounding* you all the time
now, so I'm. . .

JOHN . . . it's alright . . .

GINGER We can do the tuna thing and talk later.

JOHN But that's just it! I don't wanna "talk later" about stuff—
the Jarlsberg wasn't supposed to *lead* to anything . . . it's a
meal, that's all. A *picnic*. Simple as that . . .

GINGER . . . then fine.

JOHN Well, that's the death of it right there. "Then fine."

GINGER It is what it is, John.

JOHN Yeah, great.

GINGER Exactly. (*Beat.*) Did you bring any drinks?

JOHN I have water and some kind of fruity something. It's
supposed to be healthy. (*He holds up both.*) Which?

GINGER Doesn't matter. / You pick.

JOHN Right . . . / (*To himself.*) What a disaster.

GINGER If it is you're helping to create it. I just asked a simple question . . .

JOHN No, uh-uh, I'm not gonna accept that. Not *that*. I'm the one that went out at seven this morning to gather up all this crap. Go over to Walmart even and buy a *plaid* blanket so it'd all be perfect, so don't tell me that I've turned this into some kind of . . . travesty . . . here because if anybody's killing the thing it's you. Like always, it's *you*. With all your . . . *talk*. (*Grabs a drink.*) Here.

GINGER . . . thanks. (*Drinks.*) It's nice. Fizzy.

JOHN Good. It's got pear in it, I think, and other various . . . some berries, maybe.

GINGER Ahhh.

JOHN I don't—that's not why I dragged you out here, to continue the battle on some new territory, I really did wanna try . . . something. Try again or whatnot. (*Beat.*) This is me reaching out to you here, so I'm . . .

GINGER Yeah?

JOHN I am, yes.

GINGER Then thank you. I appreciate that.

JOHN Well, it's worth it to me. Obviously. And it would take a *lot*, after all the crap we've—that *I've* done—but I'm trying.

GINGER No, yeah, I can see that . . . that you're making an effort. (*Smiles.*) You usually hate *plaid*, so that must've been hard!

JOHN Ha-ha. (*Grins.*) Very funny . . .

GINGER I do get it, John. The "gesture" part of it, I'm saying. Thanks for trying . . .

JOHN My pleasure. I guess . . .

GINGER Uh-huh. (*Beat.*) And so you're not gonna answer me, then, right?

JOHN About . . . ?

GINGER You. The "what's up?" part of you.

JOHN I'm . . . I don't get it. Why do you always have to do *this*?! Huh?

GINGER Just because . . .

JOHN Yeah, that really helps. Thanks. "Just because." (*Beat.*) Why do you have to . . . *question* everything? Huh? It's not . . . I'm . . .

GINGER John . . . the whole thing I've been dealing with for years now, the "you" that gets tossed at Chrissy and me has changed in the last month or so, and frankly it unnerves me. Both of us, actually . . . (*Beat.*) There, now, how was that? Thirty seconds or so and I've said all I needed to, for me *and* her.

JOHN That's terrific.

GINGER You can say something back if you wanna.

JOHN . . . *please* . . .

GINGER I'm serious! Disagree or, or, you know . . . argue. Swear at me. I'm used to all that. But this guy . . . Mr. Happiness . . . he's . . .

JOHN Have I been *that* scary a person before? I mean, really? I'm just . . .

GINGER Sometimes, yeah. You were. (*Beat.*) I will admit that since the . . . you know . . . since what happened you've been different. *But.* You want the truth, there it is. Yes.

JOHN . . . I don't know what to say now.

GINGER There's nothing that goes with it, it's just a fact. You made me nervous. . . . as a man, as a husband. A father, even. I never felt like I could trust you . . . because of what might come out of your mouth or how you were gonna handle some situation. Physically, emotionally, all that . . . you'd suck the air out of a room when you entered it. You lied all the time, continually. As if it was *oxygen*. I have other doubts, too, about you and, and . . . but we don't have to go there . . . no sense now. (*Beat.*) Do I really need to go on? I've said all of it before, in other ways, so it's just a repeat . . .

JOHN Right. (*Beat.*) And? I mean . . .

GINGER . . . and now *this*! This other guy who takes me out with a blindfold on into the woods and is helping me over *logs* and putting a coat down for me to sit on! Now, who the *hell* is that guy? Don't you figure I'd be a little, you know . . . curious? And I don't know *him*, either, if I can trust him, if this is just some act, or if it's . . . what?

JOHN It's not! It's just . . . me. The "new" me, I mean. Someone I discovered in all the—I dunno, whatever. In whatever happened.

GINGER . . . listen to yourself . . .

JOHN I can't explain it! I'm . . . it's . . . imagine a light that's been . . . some switch that . . . no, that's not it, not a switch, but a . . . this moment of truth. A second that comes to you with glaring lights and, and . . . it sounds crazy, I know . . . but it happened.

GINGER What?

JOHN I dunno! I've had a . . . something. A thing. I've already told you. (*Beat.*) I'm a "new" man now, and I'm . . . I'm just . . .

GINGER Okay. (*Points.*) Can I have the carrot sticks there . . . ?

JOHN Sure. It's called "crudite" or something. On the little sign-thingie, I mean.

GINGER Ohhhh, really? That just means they can charge you an extra five bucks for it . . .

JOHN Probably!

A moment of peace between them. GINGER *sips on her drink and tries a carrot.*

JOHN It's . . . Ginger, I've changed. Really. I mean it this time . . .

GINGER "Changed" like how? What're you . . . ?

JOHN Just . . . you know. Changed. I'm not, like, a college professor, I don't know all the words for it, but this thing came over me and I'm . . . it's . . . ahh, forget it! I dunno.

GINGER No, I wanna hear this . . . specifically, I mean. What's changed? (*Beat.*) John?

JOHN *Me!* As a person. As a human being I have undergone some . . . it's hard to put it into simple terms.

GINGER Well, try. Seriously. I'm a *simple* gal. Is it inside, in your head, or has it . . . ?

JOHN I feel *lighter.* Not just the . . . light of Christ or anything, but freer . . . I have a testimony now. I'm converted, in a way.

GINGER So you say. I'd like you to explain it.

JOHN I don't know! It was, like . . . this flash and bright *things* or whatever. It was . . . this'll sound just goofy but for a moment I felt as if I'd been lifted up . . . I mean, literally *off* the ground . . . like Saul on the road to *Damascus*, or, or . . . you know?

GINGER Who? / Okay, seriously, you are spooking the shit outta me here, John! What does that even mean? "Saul?"

JOHN Honey, come on! / You've heard of him. I'm sure you have . . . Christmas mass and things like that. / We used to go sometimes.

GINGER No. / Yeah, but I wasn't listening! I used to balance my *checkbook* . . .

JOHN Ging . . .

GINGER I'm serious! And you—John, you're always dead asleep during that crap. (*Beat.*) *What* is all this?! I'm not kidding now.

JOHN Honey, I've had a sort of . . . this kind of, I don't know the name of it! I've become enlightened, I guess. That's what people call it these days . . . "faith" or whatever. I have faith in a higher . . . in God. In the *idea* of a God. Yeah. I now have this . . .

GINGER . . . "faith." Huh. (*Beat.*) And . . . Jesus, I don't even know what to say to you . . . (*Thinks.*) Not "Jesus," I suppose. Right?

JOHN Not if you don't have to, but hey . . . I'm not gonna be a freak about it. Honestly.

GINGER Oh, well, that's *comforting* . . .

JOHN I'm really not! Promise. (*Beat.*) This'll all take time and I'm prepared for that. (*Beat.*) But I think that we need to have another "go" at it. / Us. As a couple. We should be going through this together, in public. Building up our . . . our . . . whole . . .

GINGER Excuse me? / . . . I'm sorry, I'm not . . .

JOHN That's what the spirit inside me's been saying. To me. / Yes. (*Beat.*) I also feel like I should buy this piece of land and we should maybe . . . build a house here.

GINGER Oh, I see. The spirit inside you . . . / *Who*?

JOHN *Us*. As family—so we can all reconnect. On a spiritual level, too, I'm saying.

GINGER What're you . . . ? You mean *all* of us, like, me and Chrissy? (*Beat*.) You're not saying that we should become some . . . are you?

JOHN Of course, but very casually. I know that it's gonna take some doing. I understand.

GINGER Oh, you do? / Great. That's really . . .

JOHN Yes. / Absolutely, I do. Sure.

GINGER And that'd make us, what? Some sort of a "Christian" or, I dunno . . . "born again" or what? / I don't even know what to call *you* now. What this is that you're . . .

JOHN Well, you'd both be . . . / It doesn't have to have a label. Does it? I mean . . .

GINGER It'd help, yeah.

JOHN Okay, fine, I'm sure there's a . . . some . . .

GINGER Do you even *know*? I mean, really? Or is this just . . . some part of your recovery from the . . . you know . . . from all that . . . ?

JOHN Of course I do! (*Smiles*.) You've waited a long time for me to come around, to be a proper—all the things you've wanted from me in this marriage and now here I am a "new" man / I am, though! I'm better.

GINGER Stop saying that. / You keep going on . . .

JOHN I am, Ginger! Honestly. And I'm prepared to try again. For you. Give you the time to change. It's all about a give-and-take, right? It is. It's a, a, a balance.

GINGER Right, but John, we're not even . . . / Yeah?

JOHN So, do it at your own pace! It's the only way to find peace,

I think . . . / It really is. I found it through love. A complete sense of freedom through absolute love . . .

GINGER   Huh. "Love." So that's how you did it?

JOHN   Pretty much. I mean . . .

GINGER   And, so, this is what . . . you're saying to me—we should try again. As man and wife? That you and I—because that's what I'm sure I heard a few seconds ago, that you want to be together again—to marry me and give this another . . . some sorta . . .

JOHN   No, it's . . . I mean, I dunno! I'm trying to listen to God. That's all. / To what he's telling me to do! Why is that so . . . ?

GINGER   Oh shit. / You're not honestly gonna keep going out there, I mean, in *public* . . . and saying stuff like that, are you?

JOHN   Yes—maybe. I dunno! What would be wrong about it if I did? Huh? / Ginger, stop . . .

GINGER   About a million things. / Maybe more.

JOHN   We're supposed to be together!! That is what he's told me, in prayer. *Yes.* That we should be a family and living under a single roof again. He did. (*Beat.*) So.

GINGER   . . . amazing . . .

JOHN   Yes. That we should use all this money I keep receiving for "good" and that we should . . . that this piece of land is where we need to start over. You and I. (*Beat.*) Ginger, I am not making this up! Why would I? No, I hear a . . . there was this . . .this voice and it . . .it told me . . .

GINGER *stands up and brushes herself off. Gets her purse, rummages through it. She produces a set of car keys.*

GINGER Great. So now you hear *voices* . . .

JOHN Honey, what're you doing?

GINGER I'm taking the car, John. *I* need to get back to, you know . . . the real world. To Civilization. *Earth.* (*Beat.*) You scare me now—worse than ever before. I wish you were a serial killer. I do. That you'd been found to be living some double life with *girls* chained up in a basement. Or a war criminal—I don't care how many women you'd raped or children or *Jews* that you might've killed . . . any of that shit would be easier to understand than this. And I mean that, as nutty as it sounds. (*Beat.*) God doesn't mean anything to us anymore. He's the boogeyman, that's all. Someone that parents use to scare their children into doing what they want 'em to do. It's the truth, John—it's not comforting, I'm not happy when you say this shit to me . . . when we die, we die. That's it. No Jesus, no heaven. It's bullshit and I knew it at *six.* We do what we do, we make *choices* and we're responsible—you were a shitty husband and now you're sorry. Some man, he put a gun in your face and now you're feeling bad about your life and you wanna change it. Fine. *Do* something. *Change* how you live the rest of it but that doesn't mean God is divine and he spoke to you . . . that is a crock of shit and you know it! In your heart? You *know* that . . . just be a *man* and say so. Go out and spread the Gospel of "I used to be a motherrfucking asshole." Try that. Or ask my forgiveness for how you treated me and we'll be even. (*Beat.*) I don't need money. I do not need all this *crap* you're doing here. No, I don't. An apology would be enough . . .

She finishes and looks at JOHN. *He tries to hold her look but it's not easy.*

JOHN I'm . . . I didn't expect you to believe me! Not at first. / I didn't! This isn't . . .

GINGER John. / *Don't.*

JOHN But, Ginger, listen, please. Please! This is not some, some, some . . . *game*, it's not. I've been . . . He spoke to me, he did. Over all the others that day . . . God came to *me* and he . . . he said that I should . . . we need to give this another chance! We *have* to!

During this JOHN *gets to his feet and presses in on her, trying to hug her. She fights back, pushing him away.*

GINGER *No.* (*Beat.*) I'm driving Chrissy to soccer at four, so—sit here and stuff your face or you can come with me. Either way is fine. (*Pointing.*) And I would dye it back if I were you—it makes you look old. And tired.

GINGER *turns and leaves.* JOHN *sits alone on the blanket.*

JOHN Ginger? Sweetie? (*To himself.*) Oh God . . .

JOHN *stands now, looking around. Hoping for* GINGER *to return.*

A burst of intense light carries us on to:

A television studio. Two chairs on a small stage with a shiny set behind them. A coffee table.

JOHN seated next to a chipper female HOST. JOHN, *dressed in a shirt and tie, looks relatively uncomfortable.*

A set of lights come up and the HOST *smiles out toward an unseen audience and cameras.*

HOST   . . . and hello again! Thank you for coming back to what is shaping up to be, well, a fascinating hour. If you're just about to join us, thanks for stopping in, for those of you who've been with us—I can't imagine that you're not as transfixed by all this as I am. (*Turns.*) Hello there and welcome back, John Smith.

JOHN   Thanks. Thank you.

HOST   I'm sure all of this must be pretty strange to you . . . / It must be.

JOHN   It is. Yes. / It's . . .

HOST   Have you ever been on TV before?

JOHN   Ummmm, no. Wait. Yes. This one time. My Little League team went to Nationals and I was the, you know . . . our spokesperson.

HOST   Really? / That's terrific.

JOHN   It's true. I was the pitcher, so . . . / Yep. They had me do most of the talking.

HOST   Wonderful! (*Smiles.*) But never like this, never the subject of an interview, or the topic of an investigative piece . . . ?

JOHN   Oh, no. Of course not. / Never.

HOST   I see. / And yet here you are . . .

JOHN Yeah, well—you know what happened. We've talked about it. / A *lot!*

HOST Absolutely we have. / Yes. And calls.

JOHN Yep. That, too.

HOST Are you comfortable yet? Speaking about it all, I mean . . . the . . .

JOHN Not really. / I dunno. It's . . .

HOST Of course. How could you be? / And yet . . . people have a fascination—some might say a "morbid" fascination—with this kind of thing. / Catastrophe.

JOHN That's true. / Uh-huh.

HOST With death and gunfire and heartbreak.

JOHN I suppose. (*Beat.*) Do you think?

HOST Absolutely. In *this* country? Oh yes.

JJOHN Yeah, probably so.

HOST Oh, John, I know so. I *know* it! (*Smiles.*) I've been doing this for a few years now and I can promise you one thing: for some reason, people eat this up. It's a sickness, but it's a national sickness so we all feel pretty okay about it . . . (*Beat.*) We are drawn to the horrible and miserable, we *thrive* on the despair of others . . . It's like a drug but it doesn't cost a dime.

JOHN Huh. Not me.

HOST Excuse me?

JOHN I said "not me." I've never been one to, you know . . . whatever. Read that stuff. To watch it on the television.

HOST No?

JOHN Not really. My wife used to, but she's . . .

HOST What? Your wife is . . . ?

JOHN I don't know anymore. She's not my, you know. We're not married so I don't know what she watches . . .

HOST I see. I'm sorry. / Right.

JOHN It's whatever. I made a lot of mistakes but I'd rather not . . . / It happens.

HOST It does, absolutely it does—and more and more often these days.

JJOHN That's what they say.

HOST I've said it myself. Right from this very seat! / It's true. Over fifty percent of marriages in this country fail. It's a fact and a shame, isn't it? Yes . . .

JOHN I'm sure you have. / That is a shame. *Fifty percent.*

HOST *Over.* (*Beat.*) But people also appreciate the positive. The *amazing.* Miracles . . . (*Beat.*) John, we've talked about that day, about the photo, even a bit about your life after the events of that shocking Thursday—but another thing happened to you that day, didn't it? Something else.

JOHN Yes. (*Beat.*) I was . . . yes. It did.

HOST Yes. Something that has come to define you as a person now—as a man, a father, a person of business.

JOHN I'm . . . I was . . .

HOST You were touched, weren't you? By a kind of . . . what? / A light and a voice . . . ? Was there something in that room with you . . . ?

JOHN This . . . it was a sort of . . . / yes . . .

HOST I don't want to put words in your mouth, but . . . (*Shuffles cards.*) It says here . . .

JOHN No, that's close to what . . . it was . . .

HOST . . . by the hand of God, you once described it as . . . this happened to you on that day, in the middle of what is now seen as the blackest day in the history of domestic violence as related to an office setting. *Thirty*-seven people dead. And you alone, unscathed.

JOHN Well . . . my ankle was scraped but . . . yeah.

HOST And you have become, for better or worse, a man of God. Of faith. Is that right?

JOHN I have, yes.

HOST But not after the fact. Not months later when you were safely at home or anything like that, right?

JOHN No, it was during. / Right.

HOST *During* the shooting. / The carnage. (*Beat.*) You fell to your knees—I have your own description of it from an official police transcript—you were "on my knees when it happened and I was blinded by a vision of light." (*Stops reading.*) Is that correct? God *lifted* you up and filled you with the spirit of, of his—am I *right* about this?

JOHN You are, yes. (*Beat.*) I don't know why you're smiling . . .

HOST Because we're on TV, John. So, what kind of light was it? / Yes? Go on.

JOHN It was like . . . / I dunno, I mean, it . . . was so . . . bright. I couldn't . . .

HOST And so this is me, Jenny Claflin, and I am being devil's advocate here: could it not have been something other that God? I mean, isn't it possible? / Helicopters?

JOHN No, I mean, it was . . . / How do you mean?

HOST The light. A spotlight. Or even the sun, maybe.

JOHN It was . . . no, there was this . . . I mean, I don't know how to describe it, but . . . no. And why would spotlights . . . if the sun . . . ?

HOST Follow me here, because I wanna believe you, John. I do. I want nothing more. To believe. It's sexy. But it's also hard to do. Isn't it? Today. It's a tough age to believe in anything, and, well, if it's something about God, then, it is almost impossible. We've all become so cynical and troubled and, and unwell. *And* we hate it when somebody else has the answers . . . when and if they're doing okay. We hate it! So then there's that. We want to believe but we don't want to believe *you*—"you" being anyone we know, not just you, John. No offense. (*Beat.*) I wonder why that is. (*Remember to look at the audience . . .*)

JOHN Probably because . . . you know . . . it's . . .

HOST What, John? Tell us.

JOHN Because it . . . it's a new, I mean . . . this doesn't happen every day. To people. So it's, I dunno, hard to swallow, I guess. When some guy like me—this nobody—comes along and says, "Hey, God spoke to me." (*Beat.*) I don't know if I'd believe in it, either, if I heard it on the news. But it did happen. And it's true. So. (*Beat.*) It is not something you'd ask for, believe me! I'm finding it very . . . it's *rough* . . . I've had to move into a different home, I'm constantly being followed, *touched.* People seem to, I dunno, want a piece of me, as if I can . . . but I'm not that guy, not Jesus or . . . I'm just a man who was . . . I was given this message . . . and I have to get it out . . . so the world can . . . yeah.

HOST Interesting. Hmmmm. (*Beat.*) Again, devil's advocate here. Prove it.

JOHN I'm sorry?

HOST You've talked to God. Prove it. *Show* me.

JOHN I don't know what you're asking . . .

HOST I'm asking you, here and now, in front of a fairly sizable—
if I don't mind saying—audience, prove that you've really had
an experience of the kind you suggest.

JOHN How?

HOST Exactly! (*Smiles.*) Isn't that fascinating?

JOHN I don't really . . . what is? I'm lost.

HOST You want us to believe you, don't you? I mean, that's that
idea, right John?

JOHN Of course. But not for . . . *me* . . . it's . . .

HOST In the same way that you believe. Because you really
do believe it, don't you? That something happened to you in
there. That day. That this Old Testament idea we have of a
God—the flowing beard, the shining robes, all that—that he
singled you out.

JOHN . . . yes. Of course. (*Beat.*) Why would I be here
otherwise? I mean . . . *why*? I'm . . .

HOST It's alright. I don't want you to have to defend yourself—
all I'm saying is that you're asking us to believe that you had
a convert experience at a moment when people all around
you—good people, men and women with families, many with
very strong Christian backgrounds—these folks were dying.
Being hunted down and shot by a madman, and during that
same moment, a man of no significant religious or moral
background is singled out by God to live and to spread his
glorious word to all of the unenlightened after his rescue.
John? Is that correct?

JOHN That's not exactly . . . / I mean, yes, I was chosen to . . .
but. Yeah. Basically. That's how it happened. (*Beat.*) Yes.

HOST Isn't that true? / Amazing. Honestly.

JOHN Thank you.

HOST It thrills me, a story like yours.

JOHN It's . . .

HOST I'm *thrilled* by the ironies and, and . . . the improbabilities of it. How nearly impossible it is, that this could ever happen in this day and age. (*Beat.*) And yet. And *yet*. It could. It just might—God *might* still work in mysterious ways. And *that's* what keeps drawing us back.

JOHN What do you mean?

HOST Just this: it doesn't really matter in the end what happened to you in there that day, John, because we can't prove it one way or the other. If we choose to believe you then we do. If not, we never will. And that, my friends (*turns to camera*) is the true meaning of faith.

JOHN I'm . . . what're you saying? / No, but . . . I . . .

HOST I'm saying I believe you, John. / I believe in you even though your story sounds like a bunch of horseshit—I can't say that so it'll get buzzed out later—but honestly, your story is incredibly hard to take in any serious way and yet. And *yet*. I want to believe you. I *choose* to. It's a little like Pascal's wager, isn't it?

JOHN I don't know what that means . . .

HOST Plus you've got a nice face, for an older guy. So . . . (*Beat.*) What's he look like, John?

JOHN Who?

HOST You know. Come on . . .

JOHN I never said I *saw* him . . . the glow was . . .

HOST Not even for a second or . . . in the light there . . . ?

JOHN No. Not a face. He isn't this . . . / Some . . .

HOST What? / Not what? Tell us . . .

JOHN He's not, like, this *body* or anything, I don't think . . . /

Because I was . . . there was light and everything, a kind of . . . but he wasn't standing there. Not like a person.

HOST How do you know? I mean, if you haven't seen him. / He could be anything, then . . . I mean, if you didn't see him. Maybe he looks like we always see him in picture books. Or Dick Van Dyke. Personally I'm hoping he looks like that—I'd feel much less intimidated if he was more like a Rob Petrie type. Kind of funny, easygoing. Falls over the thing there, in the living room. (*To* JOHN.) What's it called? The, you know, the footrest-thing . . . they have a name. / Oh, come on! It's . . .

JOHN I dunno. / I'm sorry, I don't know . . .

HOST Doesn't matter. Just funny. (*Beat.*) So no face on this God of yours, hmmmm? He did not manifest himself in any real . . . what? / Tell me. What? As a series of . . .

JOHN No, He was a . . . this sort of . . . / He's not like you or me, obviously . . . he's . . .

HOST You're sure it was a "he?" All sorts of ladies out there— the Gloria Steinems and Germaine Greer types—they'll be all over this in the morning . . .

JOHN Yes. I heard his voice. He was a man.

HOST Fine. Just asking. (*Whispers.*) You know how we ladies can get! We can be *awfully* territorial when it comes to power . . .

JOHN I guess. You're just joking with me now, right?

HOST I am, yes. But not making fun. There's a difference. / Good. Just so you do.

JOHN I know./ I do. It's okay.

HOST Thank you. For understanding . . . (*Smiles.*) John, God spoke to you—reached out and he made contact with *you*— as I said, I believe it because I want to. Fine. So tell me, here in front of our audience, what did he say to you? At that moment of doubt and fear? Alarms are going off and it's . . . you have this *killer* still on the loose and you're crouching down . . . (*Beat.*) What did he say?

JOHN He told me . . . God said to me that I should try to . . . that I needed to be good. / That we should try and be good. To each other.

HOST . . . excuse me? / "Good?"

JOHN Yes. You know, like . . . kind.

HOST That's it? That you should be . . . what?

JOHN No, that we all did. We *all* need to be . . .

HOST We should be, what, good people? / Yeah? Even the Muslims? Because *somebody* needs to have a serious talk with those guys . . . (*Beat.*) I'm joking!

JOHN Yes. / Or better. Better than we are. That is what he was telling me—he told me to stay where I was, down on my knees . . .

HOST Show me. How it was . . . if you would.

JOHN Hmmmm?

HOST Can you . . . ? (*Indicates.*) Get down and show me how you were. What it was like.

JOHN Here? You mean . . . in front of everybody?

The female HOST *nods.* JOHN *hesitates but then gets out of his chair and drops to the carpet. Gets on his knees.*

JOHN Like this—I was down on the floor like this here.

HOST And he spoke to you?

JOHN *looks up at her and nods. His face is open and as earnest as a young child's.*

The HOST *smiles down at him and scoots to the end of her chair. Watching. Indicates for him to continue.*

JOHN   Yes. Just like that. I could . . . it was so hot in there, and bright . . . the police had made it inside the room and I could hear a bunch of voices, like, on the radio and from outside . . . the sound of copters going overhead . . . and I was, I was trying to get to a safe place but he said to me, God is talking to me at that moment and he says, "Don't move. Stay where you are. All will be well and tomorrow go spread my gospel of goodness. That all men should work at this, that goodness is all that matters." (*Beat.*) I'm paraphrasing, of course, but it was basically that. / And he wanted me to go spread it . . . this message of good will.

HOST   I see. / Wow. That's . . . it really comes down to that, huh? Just . . . being "good?" (*Smiles.*) Don't even have to worry about taxes, huh? Just-be-good.

JOHN   I don't . . . I can only say what I heard.

HOST   I suppose that's true. / So . . .

JOHN   Yeah. / I mean . . .

HOST   You lived so you could tell us that. (*She imitates* JOHN.) "Be good now."

JOHN   Something like that . . .

HOST   I see. (*Bigger this time.*) "Hey everybody, be good!" (*To* JOHN.) Sort of like a game-show host or something. / "WELL HEY THERE, FOLKS! Just keep on being good, okay!!"

JOHN   What do you mean? / No, not like . . .

HOST It's a little simplistic, isn't it?

JOHN No, it's not simplistic . . . I'll tell you what it is—it's *simple*. That's what.

HOST What is? (*Beat.*) It's simple to be good?

JOHN Yeah, it is. It's just a choice.

HOST Well, I think about three-quarters of my viewing audience would probably disagree with you, John, but . . .

JOHN Because they're weak. Like I was. I would always choose the easy way out. The quick and safe path. Don't stand out and do not make waves. It's . . . you know what, it's much easier to do the wrong thing or make bad choices . . . it is. Who cares anymore?

HOST . . . well, somebody must . . . (*To camera.*) In fact, that's a great call-in question for a bit later in the show. Let's hear from some viewers: "Hey you out there, do you think that anyone really cares? Do *you*?"

JOHN All we want to do is get to the end. Most of us. Live life and get whatever we can for ourselves and screw anybody who gets in the way. We don't do crimes because we don't want to get caught, go to jail, get raped by some prisoner . . . not because it's a sin. Because we *shouldn't*. (*Beat.*) Being good is hard. I couldn't do it before, back when I was married and just living my life, it was almost impossible!! I did all kinds of crap every day that I'm ashamed of and got away with but that's not me now. God told me "no." He spoke right to me—you make light of it if you want, but—this voice as clear as you or I talking reached out and saved me and let me know what I need to be doing on earth. Life, it is precious, it's short and, and can be the most *amazing* . . . but you have to work at it! You have to appreciate people and you have to do good. Good, brave things and so that's . . . I'm . . . I do that now.

HOST Well, I certainly know what you mean . . . "prison rape" is definitely on my list of bad things, too! Morning breath. Ummmmm, FACEBOOK. Oh, and *sloth*—I am *im*possible at getting up in the morning!! (*Smiling.*) So, John, let's try and . . . (*startled*) An "ottoman!" That's the . . . the foot-thingie, that's what they're called. An ottoman. Thank God! I'm so glad I thought of that!

JOHN *gets up, standing instead of sitting in his chair.*

HOST John . . . you're not in our shot anymore.

JOHN Excuse me?

HOST You need to sit down. / John, we can't get both of us in the frame if you're . . .

JOHN No, I don't . . . / I see what you're doing now. You're just making fun of me.

HOST No, John, I'm not doing that—it's just a bit hard to swallow, you know? All this.

JOHN Then don't. Don't swallow it. That's up to you . . . / It's the word of God. Do with it whatever you want. (*Beat.*) I'm going.

HOST Don't leave. That's not the way to . . . / You can't just leave!

JOHN Good-bye. / Yes, I can. Watch me.

HOST John, please just sit down and we'll . . . / We should go to a commercial . . . can we . . . ?

JOHN No. This is . . . just stop! *No.* (*Beat.*) Look, we're all searching, every day people are out there trying to find the, you know . . . answers, the *big* answer to what's wrong in their lives. *Every*body is! It's not just me—I've had people spit on me and others chase me down the street, just to hold my hand. (*Beat.*) I didn't want this. I was at work, just doing my job and this thing happened. A guy went nuts shooting people and I survived. I got through it and I'm okay. I took a photo but I didn't . . . I don't even know what I'm saying now, but God spoke to me, he choose right then to take charge of my life and so be it! You think that's crazy . . . how 'bout Noah? And Moses? Or Adam and goddamn *Eve*? Huh? Read the Koran or the Bible or any of it. *All* of this is crazy! Every last guy in the belly of a *whale*'s insane. Okay? Totally bonkers . . . but it's also *true*. (*Beat.*) So I don't care if you're not . . . just forget it. This is bullshit.

JOHN *walks off.* HOST *is left sitting in her chair.*

HOST I can't believe he's . . . "bullshit," huh? Well, that's not very Christ-like, now, is it? (*Smiles.*) That's okay, folks, that is alright. We'll buzz that out later—you'll never know we had a problem. Join us tomorrow when we visit with two transsexuals who are both suing the state of California for the right to sunbathe topless. (*Tries to hold her smile.*) Can somebody—are you gonna stop rolling or what? I mean, Jesus Christ—can we *please* go to break here, or . . . ? (*Beat.*) *Please?*

The TV HOST *stares out toward the darkened auditorium.*

A burst of intense light carries us on to:

A bed. A man is face down and naked, save for a few bits of well-placed leather. He is gagged and tied. Ass up in the air. Full mask over his head.

A woman in a leather outfit is next to him—this is DIVA MIDNIGHT. *She whips him slowly and repeatedly. He flinches each time. After a while he holds up a hand and signals to her. Garbled speech.*

She comes over, removes his mask and his gag. He looks up at her. It is JOHN SMITH, *looking a little dazed.*

DIVA   . . . speak now.

JOHN   Owww. (*Beat.*) I mean . . .

DIVA   Does that hurt, my pet?

JOHN   Yeah, it kinda does. Ooohhh. Yes.

DIVA   Do you like that? / You don't?

JOHN   Ummmm, no, not really. No. / It, ummm, stings so it's not . . .

DIVA   What?

JOHN   It, ahhhh . . . it hurts? Like, ouch?

DIVA   Hurts what?

JOHN   Ummmmmm . . . I dunno, I'm confused . . . hurts *me*?

DIVA   Yes. And? / *And*?

JOHN   And . . . and . . . it hurts me a *lot* . . . ?/ Like, more than I want it to? I'm not sure what you're driving at . . . here . . .

A quick snap from the whip across JOHN's *ass. He jerks to attention. He yells out.*

DIVA "It hurts, *Mistress*."

JOHN Oh, sorry, that's right . . . "it hurts, Mistress." (*Cringes.*) Wow. *Damn* . . . that thing really packs a, you know . . . / Owww. Punch. I guess.

DIVA No, what? / Yes.

JOHN *turns on his side a bit, toward the woman as he tries to protect himself a moment.*

JOHN Can we just . . . ?

DIVA What?

JOHN Ummm . . . like, take a rest here for a sec? Hold off on the . . . all of the whacking for a minute? (*Beat.*) I'm kinda . . . I couldn't use that code word—what's it called? The "safe" word—because your gag was so . . .

DIVA Is that what you want? To stop?

JOHN I'm . . . just for a . . . it was hard to breath in there. And that zipper was kinda . . .

DIVA I thought you wanted me to control you—to not care what you wanted? Hmmm?

JOHN Yeah, no, I did say that, you're right, when I came . . . I wanted to try something that was, you know, like this. A bit more *extreme* to see if God would still . . . see if he'd still speak to me . . . / Yes, and . . .

DIVA *God*?/ Oh. (*Beat.*) And so? So? Did he?

JOHN I just . . . I don't mean stop the clock or anything like that . . . I'll just . . . I need, like, a breather, alright? Because this may be the wrong . . . sort of . . . ahhhh . . . / This feels more like . . . a *sin* now. This.

JOHN *scrambles for a moment, trying to think of the right word.*

DIVA I'm listening . . . / Ahh. I see.

JOHN I mean, I'm sure you're good at it . . . doing it the right way and everything, but it's not—this isn't doing what I thought it might do. For me.

DIVA No?

JOHN Uh-uh. I was sort of hoping for . . . I dunno, but the handcuffs are starting to pinch a little and—*okay*—and, ummm, I wanted to dare myself . . . with all this stuff you've been doing to me, but I never thought it through, I guess. Not completely, anyway, and I just feel like maybe it's not . . . you know . . . it's not for me to test God. Or my faith. (*Beat.*) It was a moment of weakness for me, of *lust*, and, and old habits that bubbled up, but I just . . . now I feel . . .

DIVA Yes? / Tell me.

JOHN I dunno . . . / Ashamed. Or something. Of *me*.

DIVA You do?

JOHN Uh-uh. Because I'm a new man. Yes.

DIVA Yes what?

JOHN "Yes, Mistress?"

DIVA Very good. (*Beat.*) And yet here we are . . .

She snaps her whip through the air for emphasis. Crack!

DIVA Are you sure we've never done this before now? You seem very familiar . . . (*Pinches him.*) . . . with this.

JOHN Aaaahhh! "Thank you, Mistress." (*Beat.*) But, see . . . about that?

DIVA Yes?

JOHN   Umm, the thing is . . . I mean, how I came to find your personal ad in that magazine? Is this . . .

DIVA   I'm listening. (*Checks watch.*) For another ten minutes . . .

JOHN   Right, right—so, look, I did want to see if I'd have any more attraction to . . . *this* again. / Yes. This isn't . . . I'm not a first-timer. Not at *this*—I don't mean, like, chains or *peeing* on each other—I haven't done that but I've gone to women before. Paid. (*Beat.*) And your ad made me curious.

DIVA   "Again?"/ About what, my pet?

JOHN   A kind of darker lifestyle—after what's happened to me, I thought it'd be, like, challenging to try this—It's not always been easy for me to open up with people in my ordinary life so it . . . seemed kinda logical to try this . . . something off the beaten path and in private. Like yourself or some person who would . . . what you do. Who does things. To men.

JOHN *glances over at her to see how that landed. Waits.*

DIVA   "Things?"

JOHN   Yes. Things. Help me understand myself . . . *about* myself. Who I am. Or used to be.

DIVA   I don't follow.

JOHN   I was . . . I used to maybe . . . (*Beat.*) I was someone who probably used women before. Back when I was—earlier in my life. So.

DIVA   I see. / Yes.

JOHN   Got massages or, saw, ladies who . . . I also did a *lot* of porno. Understand? / You do?

She reaches over and rubs the whip across his back—over and around JOHN's *body. Caressing him.*

JOHN I'm . . . please don't hit me again . . .

DIVA Why did you come here, then? Tell me that, before your hour is up . . .

JOHN I'm . . . I needed to . . .

DIVA Tell your Mistress. Why-are-you-here?

*She raises up the whip again—*JOHN *flinches and reacts.*

JOHN Okay, okay! Look, I came here to . . . because of two things . . . like I said, to test myself and see if I felt any . . . you know . . . *draw* again . . . / *And* because I knew your mother.

DIVA Yes, and? *And*? / . . . excuse me? *What*?

Her voice is different and her whole demeanor is changed. She is now just a concerned young woman. She stares over at him.

JOHN I was . . . I worked with her. At Sanford-Gross. We were both very . . . *yes.*

DIVA I see. So, you're . . . are you trying to get me to sign that . . . ? / You are, aren't you?

JOHN No. / *No*, of course not! This has nothing to do with the court case. That's a civil thing. Honestly. I'm just here because . . .

DIVA . . . oh, my God . . . then why would you . . . ? (*Stops.*) *That's* where I know you from! On the TV. You're that . . . oh, God . . .

JOHN I didn't know how to approach you! One of my other colleagues, a woman from the sales department, Mrs. Reynolds, do you know her? Dolores Reynolds? / A redhead? She was sick that day and . . . it doesn't matter. She had your number, so I . . .

DIVA Maybe . . . / My mom was . . . she knew a lot of, I mean, she had friends all over . . .

JOHN I would never do this normally, come here to where you . . . *work* . . . and do all this . . . but I went through that whole thing, too, and I'm really struggling . . . / Can you . . . ?

JOHN *indicates toward the bondage devices. She responds.*

DIVA Oh. I see. / Sorry. Here, let me . . .

She pulls JOHN *upright. He staggers to his feet in all his handcuffs and leg chains and spiked collar glory. He's quite a sight. She releases him from his bonds.*

JOHN I was actually talking to her, your mom, maybe an hour before it all happened . . .

DIVA Really? / Wow, that's . . . *really*? She did?

JOHN Yeah, a lovely person, always upbeat and very happy. Had pictures of you out there on her desk . . . / Oh yeah! Right when I saw you I recognized you—even with the whip.

DIVA I'm surprised. We didn't always get along because of . . . you know. Partly this.

JOHN Well, she spoke highly of you. Very.

DIVA Huh. Okay, so . . . that's . . . ummm . . .

Her eyes well up a bit and she crosses the room to get a Kleenex.
JOHN *quickly pulls on his street clothes.*

JOHN I'm the guy who took the picture. (*Beat.*) You've no doubt
seen it . . . that was me in there, who did that.

She turns to JOHN, *looking him up and down. Silent for the
moment.*

DIVA Oh. / So, I mean . . . *you* did all that? The snapshot?

JOHN Yeah. / I did, yes. (*Beat.*) I'm trying to go see as many
people—families of the deceased as I can so that I'm . . .
people need to understand that I was just . . .

DIVA She was in there. / My mom.

JOHN I know. / Yes, that's why I . . . that's . . .

DIVA You took a photo of her. Dead.

JOHN It wasn't . . . no . . . I didn't know what I was doing . . .
it was happening so fast and I just kept . . . I was *crawling*
along . . .

DIVA . . . and you stopped to take that picture? With her body
all . . . like that?

JOHN Yes, but not for any . . . I thought maybe later that
families might—it was the gunman that I . . . that's why I took
it. Because of him. (*Beat.*) I'm sorry . . .

DIVA I see. (*Beat.*) I dunno what else to say.

JOHN I really am. Honestly . . . (*Beat.*) I thought that people
would want to know the truth. The story of that day . . . you
know? / After it was all over. But I never . . .

DIVA Okay. / And all that money? I know you sold it, so . . .
that's . . .

JOHN It mostly went to charity and to, to . . . a bunch of . . . various . . . things like that.

DIVA I see. "Mostly."

JOHN I also came to give you some . . . I mean, out of what's left of the . . . I'd like to give you it to you. If it would help.

DIVA Help what?

JOHN I don't know, I'm just . . . to start a . . .

DIVA You're not going to insult me now, are you?

JOHN . . . no . . .

DIVA About my life and who I am, what I do or shit like that?

JOHN No, of course not. I just thought it . . .

DIVA It won't bring her back. Will it?

JOHN It can't, no . . . but I just . . . I thought if we could talk then maybe you'd see that I was . . . / You'd see that I cared about her, about . . .

DIVA What? / About my mom? You did?

JOHN Absolutely yes! I had lunch with her many times . . . over the years? A *lot* of times . . . we were friendly. On good, good terms.

DIVA Okay. Well, that's nice to know.

JOHN Janice was my friend. She really was.

DIVA Yeah? / Ummmm, no. Please don't.

JOHN Yes, Jill. She was . . . (*Beat.*) May I call you that? "Jill?" / I'm sorry?

DIVA I'd rather that you . . . they don't know my real name here and we're not acquainted. I don't know you, Mr. . . . ? (*Stares at him.*) Although, yeah, I do recognize you now. From the news and, like, magazines . . .

JOHN I'm Mr. Smith. John. / What did I . . . ?

DIVA Mr. Smith, look, you are not anybody to me, so please
don't do that again . . . / Use my name.

JOHN But I was—I know we got off on the wrong foot here with
all the . . . but please . . .

DIVA I'm sorry, our session is over. There's a shower next door.
Towel is complimentary. (*Beat.*) I hope you enjoyed yourself
today and will return to Tina's Dungeon in the very near
future . . .

She looks at him but doesn't leave. She hovers.

DIVA I'll see you in front. (*Waits.*) Let me ask you something,
though, and think about it before you answer me. Before you
go. Are you sure she was dead, when you took that picture?/
Was-my-mom-dead?/ For certain?

JOHN What? / . . . yes. / Well, I mean, I didn't . . .

DIVA I know how she looked, I *know* that, but this "friend" of
yours, who you ate *so* many lunches with and was laying
there bleeding on that marble floor—you took the photo, you
lived that day, showed the world what happened there—all
important stuff. But did you stop for two seconds to see if
you could help her? My mother? Did you put your finger to her
neck and check her pulse? Did you do at least that much, Mr.
Smith? (*Beat.*) Did you?

JOHN . . . I . . . no, I didn't. / I did not. No.

DIVA No? / Huh. I wonder why . . .

She turns heel (all six inches of them) and heads off.

JOHN Mistress! / Diva Midnight!

DIVA Yes? / What is it?

JOHN *Please* . . . I know you don't owe me anything or, or know me from Adam, not really. I'm doing this thing—trying to change who I am and let the world know that—and it is really hard! You know? People don't want it, do not wanna hear it, or believe that I could be this . . . new . . . guy. But I am and I just want you to know—I'm sure she was gone . . . I'm *sure* of it! I feel completely sure . . . she was at peace and . . . that's . . . (*He holds out his hands.*) Diva, would you pray with me? Just for a moment, in the quiet of this room here . . . could we do that? Just two people who need the love of God in their hearts, might you do that with me? *Please*? (*Beat.*) I'll pay for . . .

She stares at him—he jumps up to his feet and goes to a hook on the wall where his jacket hangs. Reaches in his pocket and produces an envelope. He sits on the bed.

DIVA What's that?

JOHN It's nothing. Don't keep it if you don't want to—give it away. It's what I've . . . it's just money. It doesn't matter. Don't think of it as . . . just do what's in your heart. That's what God wants. Because he knows that if you search there—if you do it with kindness and grace—that you'll do the right thing. *Every* time. You will! (*Smiles.*) Please . . . take my hand and we can just . . . let's pray for a moment. Two of us who once were lost but now . . . please. I'm asking you with a pure heart. Please, I beg you. Please. *Please.*

DIVA *nods and takes his hand. She sits next to him. She starts to cry. He holds her as they bow in prayer.* JOHN *continues to mumble a prayer in her ear.*

JOHN   (*Building.*) Hand yourself over to him, my dear . . . do it. Do it now. Open your heart and allow the light of Christ to enter. To enter and fill you up. Let him fill you up! / Say it to him, say it now! Say "please enter my body and fill me up!!" / Let him hear you then, my child, tell him your name and let him know that you're here, that you want his love, that you need him . . . / Tell him again! Again! / And again!! Tell him who you are, my angel!!

DIVA   (*Escalating.*) Please, yes. *Please* fill me up. / Please! / My name . . . my name is Jill. I'm Jill! / Oh God, please . . . please! *Please!* I'm Jill! / I want you now! I *need you!* It's me! It's Jill! / Oh God, I'm Jill! I'm Jill! Jill!!

JOHN *and* DIVA *sit on the bed, praying and clutching each other. She is working herself into a kind of frenzy.*

A burst of intense light carries us on to:

An outdoor mall. Middle of some suburban tangle with lots of stores around and milling crowds. It's been raining.

JOHN is alone on a bench. Watching the clock. He is about to get up as a woman approaches him. This is JESSE, first cousin to Ginger.

JESSE . . . hey. Sorry. / Parking. *And* the rain.

JOHN Oh. Hi. Don't worry. / Yeah, it's . . .

JESSE The mall sucks. Especially this kind.

JOHN I know.

JESSE Why'd you pick this place? *Outdoors...*

JOHN I dunno. I just . . . (*Beat.*) Because of the press and all that, I guess. Sorry.

JESSE Yeah, well, they'll never follow you out here!

JOHN I know. (*Smiling.*) Thanks for meeting me.

JESSE Sure. (*Beat.*) Saw you on TV one night.

JOHN Great. / Ha! Terrific. It's the *hair.*

JESSE It made you look older. / Yeah, that shit is crazy! (*Beat.*) Anyway . . .

JOHN You didn't really sound like you wanted to come when I called, said you're only doing me a favor . . .

JESSE . . . I didn't know for sure. You sending me an e-mail like that. / I'm still trying to make sense of it.

JOHN Look, I . . . I don't even know how to begin this . . . / I need to come clean, I do, but I want you to do it, too. / With me.

JESSE *What?* / Are you . . . ?! *No.*

JOHN We *have* to admit it! *All* of it.

JESSE No fucking way. What're you even . . . ?

JOHN Because I don't feel good about the past. I feel like shit. And, and . . .

JESSE Okay, fine, but . . . / I hear you, but John . . .

JOHN I need to start feeling better about myself and I don't. / So *that's* why . . .

JESSE I get it, John, but I can't do this right now! (*Beat.*) I can't have this shit in my life today or, like, even soon . . .

JOHN Why not? / Isn't it better to face it, get it over with instead of being . . . all . . .

JESSE *What*? / Really, you gotta ask me that?

JOHN Yeah, I do. Yes. Tell me. *Why*?

JESSE Because we're . . . you and I have had this, like, a very serious and, and longish relationship going, without my cousin ever knowing about it. Alright?

JOHN This is what I'm talking about! She's my wife and I've been deceiving her with . . . for so long! *Forever*, and I just . . . look, I want to be honest for once . . . I'm . . .

JESSE I know, I know! But listen, what do you think the world says when they find out that you've had an affair, and I mean a prolonged thing with the cousin of your ex-wife—that this happened *before* you were divorced—you think they're gonna believe another thing you say? A *single* word that comes outta your mouth? Do you? That'll be the end of all this . . . this . . .

JOHN Who cares? / I'm different now, right?

JESSE What? / Yeah, but you're . . . you *still* . . .

JOHN I'm saying "who cares?" If it's true, I mean, if it *really* is—*if* I'm a changed person—why do I care if people think I'm a liar or not about it all?/ *I* know the truth now . . .

JESSE *Because*. / But they'll . . . people get all . . . they'll judge you! They constantly judge.

JOHN *I* know whether all that shit happened to me in there or
not. Period. So screw it. I can take what they throw at me, but
I need to release myself from the rest of it. (*Takes her hands.*)
Please understand. It's not just me asking for this . . . it's
God. It *is*. *Please*, Jesse! Let's do this. Together . . . we can
do this now, the *right* thing. We can.

JESSE *doesn't react for a moment as she studies* JOHN's *face.* JOHN
sits and waits.

JOHN   I just wanted you to hear about it from me and not have
Ginger get all . . .
JESSE   Don't say shit about her, alright? Don't start in on that or
I'm outta here, right now. I mean it. (*Beat.*) "Ginger."
JOHN   Sorry. I didn't mean to . . .
JESSE   Yeah, well, just don't. 'Kay?
JOHN   Fine. Sorry.
JESSE   Whatever. I have my own thing with her so that's my
deal—you just worry about us.
JOHN   Sure. (*Beat.*) I know that she can get in a place where she
can't help but bad-mouth me sometimes, so. That's all I'm
saying. (*Beat.*) This is me asking this, to bring us out into the
open. To put away the old.
JESSE   Fine.
JOHN   And I don't want that to be your only . . . there's a new
"me" that I want to share with you, that's all. Isn't that okay,
Jesse?
JESSE   I guess.
JOHN   I *was* gonna call you, I promise . . .
JESSE   I'll bet. / I wonder about that . . .

JOHN Honestly. / I was! / I just wanted to . . .

JESSE Yeah, when? / Next year? Or maybe . . .

JOHN I need to have time, time alone with you so that you can see this guy, get to know the man that I want to be now. For you *and* for Ginger and, you know . . . for everybody. (*Beat.*) I want this to be the start of a new thing between us all. Whatever it is that we can sort out here and not feel . . . I'm *trying*, okay? I want it to end happily if it can . . . (*Beat.*) I hope that doesn't sound weird. Does it?

JESSE Kinda.

JOHN It's not, I promise, I'm just . . . I need . . .

JESSE I mean . . . can you even hear yourself when you're talking like that or does it just, like, *leak* out of your head? How can you even say shit that is so retarded? Huh? (*Beat.*)

JOHN It's not retarded. / Stop . . .

JESSE Come sit where I am and then say that. / You should hear yourself: "end happily."

JOHN You know what? Forget it. Just screw you, Jesse. (*Beat.*) I knew this was a mistake.

JESSE Ahhhh, there's my baby! *That's* more like the John I know . . .

JOHN You're an idiot and I don't have to sit here and, and, and deal with it . . .

JESSE Never have before, why start now?! / Nah, you're more of the fuck 'em and leave 'em type, right?

JOHN Just shut up. Okay? / . . . hey, watch your . . .

*She puts her hands up in his face—*JOHN *pushes her away.*

JESSE What? You wanna hit me, too—oohhhh, it's a really special outing here today!

JOHN You're so . . . I *knew* this would happen . . .

JESSE That's right . . . / 'Course ya did.

JOHN I did know! / . . . such an asshole . . .

JESSE Yep, you've *really* changed, good for you.

JOHN You try and talk to somebody, just have a goddamn *conversation* with a person and it blows up in your face! It always does.

JESSE You're not talking with me, you're just spouting shit in my direction, telling me all your little . . . *visions* and, and . . . and you want me to make you feel better about all the bad shit we've done . . .

JOHN . . . don't worry about it . . . / Ohhh, just . . .

JESSE . . . like this is some new, amazing deal! / Don't point your finger at me! Don't!

JOHN . . . we don't need to understand each other or anything like that, we don't, we can just keep limping along pretending that we're listening, that we care! Whatever.

JESSE Exactly right, baby. Just like the little kiddies say. "Whatever."

JOHN Wow, so . . . fucking funny . . .

JESSE Boy, listen to your mouth. Huh? You don't sound so much like Jesus in his little manger now, do ya?

JOHN Don't worry about me! / Then . . . *don't*!

JESSE I don't. / I won't!!

JOHN You think a person can't *swear* and still love God, huh? Of course I can, I'm just trying to be better. You think I can't be living in his embrace but know for a fact that you are a goddamn moron? Hmmmm?! Is that what you think?!

JESSE I don't give a shit, that's what *I* think! I do not care what's going through your fucking head anymore, so there . . .

JOHN You think I can't realize that you're a *cunt*—and I don't like using that word, but—someone who wants to make trouble for her own family . . . / Who would go to somebody after messing around with the husband of her own *cousin* and then goes and make trouble when they're working to get through their problems . . . / For what? What's the *point* of that if not trouble?

JESSE Listen, you cocksucker, don't even . . . / You don't have a fucking clue about it, anything I'm saying here, so just don't! / You think you're changed, so prove it!! Show us all the amazing shit you have in your life now, go on!! Prove it!

JOHN You want . . . money or something, I suppose? Come on! Just say it! *YOU* SAY IT. SAY IT TO ME. I WANT MONEY. I WANT ALL OF YOUR MONEY OR, OR TO GET BACK AT MY FAMILY OR TO HURT SOMEBODY BECAUSE MY LIFE IS SHIT! MY LIFE IS SHIT AND I'M ANGRY!! SAY IT!!! I AM AN ANGRY, *GREEDY* LITTLE BITCH AND I ALWAYS WILL BE!!!!

They stop for a moment, both realizing again that they're in public. Silence. JESSE *finally looks up at* JOHN.

JOHN This has *always* been about using me . . . using *me* to get at her. *Always.* Why would you stop now? Huh?! WHY?!

Without warning JESSE *smacks* JOHN *across the face. Hard. Several times.*

JOHN's *eyes widen. He tenses up, like he's about to hit* JESSE; *after a moment, though, he bursts into tears. Big torrents of tears.*

Despite herself, JESSE *begins to pat* JOHN's *back.*

JOHN   . . . (*Weeping.*) Oh, Jesse, I don't know . . . I'm so lost . . . I just feel so, so . . . *I mean, I'm trying and I try but, shit, I'm just sinking out here! Can't help it . . .Help me . . .please . . .*

JOHN *puts his head down in an effort to hide his face.* JESSE *reaches out and cradles him.*

JESSE   Shh. Stop. S'okay. (*Holds him.*) You know what? As far as what happened goes, I, for one, kinda believed you. I'm serious.

JOHN   . . . yeah? (*Fighting back tears.*) Really?

JESSE   Yep. Since I first heard it. I'm the only person—on the news, mother, *everybody*—who believed you were gonna walk outta there okay.

JOHN   You did?

JESSE   Always. From the first minute.

JOHN   That's . . . huh. I'm surprised by that.

JESSE   Whatever.

JOHN   No, I don't mean . . . I just am.

JESSE   Hey, I'm a pretty positive person a lot of the time. (*Smiles.*) Every so often.

They smile at each other. Détente for a moment. Some kind of softening between them.

JOHN Yeah?

JESSE It's true . . .

JOHN I'm glad you did. That you thought that.

JESSE It was just this feeling . . . and maybe it's 'cause I need
to believe in something now too, or that I'm, I dunno, suffering
over my own shit, but I do think God came to you. I *want* to
believe it and I do. And the warmth . . . the truth of it, the
faith you have—it feels like maybe it's making me into a little
bit better of a person.

JOHN Yeah? I mean . . .God, that'd be so . . .

JESSE I can't describe it, it's just . . . this glow I've got. Every so
often, even . . . not that I'm going off to *Africa* to do nursing
or shit like that! I don't mean I'm gonna walk on water soon,
but I do feel something. Not so alone or, or . . . words suck! It
sounds stupid now.

JOHN . . . no, please . . . go on. (*Beat.*) Jesse?

JESSE I just have this sense of things... of a kind of purpose or
something. Concerning what I've done, too, which is probably
why I've been feeling the guilt and all; it's just scary so I've
been fighting it. (*Beat.*) But about you it's usually good things
in my heart. / Nice, true things.

JOHN Really? / So you feel . . . what? Tell me.

JESSE It totally overtook me. This complete . . . like, utter
sense of confidence in you . . . even when it was going on. I
absolutely knew that you'd come out of it all . . . alive. I saw
your face, up on the news there and, and I could tell you'd
been lifted up. All, like . . . overcome. (*Beat.*) I mean, check
out your fucking *hair*!

JOHN I know. It's crazy.

JESSE And look at you—you did alright. People even think you're a hero or something . . .

JOHN Ha! / Hardly.

JESSE Serious. / They do . . . some do. I've seen a few blogs on the Internet about it.

JOHN People don't know what to think . . .

JESSE Maybe.

JOHN And I understand that. If I saw my story on the news . . . I wouldn't know. / Probably think I was insane or, or . . .

JESSE I guess./ Yeah, prob'ly.

JOHN They certainly don't wanna believe the part about God, I'll tell ya that much!

JESSE Well, that figures . . . right?

JOHN I suppose.

JESSE You're one of those *20/20* type things, or CBS *48 Hours* investigations. Doesn't happen every day. You know?

JOHN True. But with the picture and all that, plus being the only person not killed . . . they've said some really mean stuff about me. In the papers and, you know. Online. (*Beat.*) *Time* magazine even called me "a charlatan." Whatever *that* means . . .

JOHN *reaches over and takes* JESSE's *hands in his. Holds them tight.*

JOHN Jess, help me prove to people that I'm . . . something. (*Beat.*) That all this . . . *amazing* stuff happened to me and nobody believes me—'cept maybe you. They don't want to or maybe afraid to. It scares them, I get that, but . . . something like this, a thing they can grasp and understand, that I'm willing to be honest about. *That's* what I need now. Proof. (*Looks at her.*) Be the proof I need, Jesse. That I've changed . . .

JESSE *places her hand on* JOHN's *knee and leaves it there.*

JESSE   . . . I'll think about it.
JOHN   Alright. So . . . then you'll . . .what ?
JESSE   I said I need to think. Okay?

They sit for a moment. Not sure what the next move is.

JESSE   . . . you used to talk about marrying me. Do you remember? In bed, you'd say that.
JOHN   I do. Yeah.
JESSE   Did you ever mean it? You always sounded like you did but that's probably easy . . . saying shit. *Meaning* it, that's tougher.
JOHN   I was . . . sure . . . when we were like that, in that *moment*, I felt like . . . you know . . .
JESSE   Don't lie if it's not true.
JOHN   I'm not. There was a time when I wanted that. I'd be with you, or sitting outside your house in my car . . . and I can remember wishing that. Yes.

She nods, looking over at him. JOHN *forces up a smile.*

JESSE   . . . and now?
JOHN   I think I'm . . . I'm just trying to get my own sense of . . . to get myself back to . . .

JESSE It's okay. I already heard that you asked Ginger back. /
You don't have to hide it.

JOHN Oh. / I wasn't sure . . . I didn't know if . . .

JESSE I just wanted to hear you say it. I guess I thought if you
had really changed, were all *strong* and high-minded and
new . . . / I thought you could say it to my face.

JOHN I'm trying to be. / That's not fair . . .

JESSE No?

JOHN It's hard. To say things like that to a person you care
about—and you do know I care for you, Jesse, I know you
do—it's very hard.

JESSE I know. I know it is, but I figured you could . . . if you
really were all different. This new and decent man of God . . .

JOHN But I'm still . . . it's still just *me*./ I'm filled with . . .
this . . . but I'm only . . . I am still the same man you knew,
only I've been . . . I'm . . .

JESSE I get it. / You're still a *guy*. And guys always wanna hide
shit. Right? / Mostly, anyways . . .

JOHN I guess we do. / Yeah. Most times.

JESSE Yep. And not any amount of God's light in this world is
gonna change that fact . . . is it now?

JESSE pats JOHN *on the cheek, then stands. He goes to get up and
hug her but she grabs his face. Kisses him hard on the mouth.*

*He tries to respond but she is already gone. Off down the hall,
drifting into the crowd.*

JOHN *looks around, starts to walk off. Returns. He sits as the sun slowly comes out. He reaches into a pocket for a pair of sunglasses. Puts them on to shield his eyes.*

After a moment, he looks up into the sky. Continues.

A burst of intense light carries us on to:

A police station. Some observation room down a hallway.

JOHN sits by himself at a desk. Cup of coffee in front of him. He gets up after a moment, walking down (toward the audience) as if to stare into a large two-way mirror.

He looks around, checks his teeth. Smiles. Frowns. Does a bit of grooming, smiles again. Last check of his teeth.

As this is going on, a male DETECTIVE enters but he goes unnoticed by JOHN for a moment. He clears his throat and JOHN whirls around. Nods at him, laughs. Points.

JOHN   . . . is there anybody out there?

DETECTIVE   Hmm? / I didn't hear what you . . .

JOHN   Sorry, I was just . . . / No, I was curious—are there, like, folks on the other side who're watching us? Looking in?

DETECTIVE   You mean in heaven? / I'm kidding. Uh-uh.

JOHN   No! Not in . . . I'm saying . . . (*Pointing.*) Out there. / Really? Nobody?

DETECTIVE   Nope. People work here. We have *work* to do, criminals to catch and kids to keep out of the hands of perverts, shit like that . . . / It's a police station, not one of those TV shows that you've been on.

JOHN   Oh. / True.

DETECTIVE   We don't have time to *watch* you. You're just a member of the public, right?

JOHN   Yes. I am.

DETECTIVE   Yeah? That's what you've been saying . . .

JOHN   I'm not anyone special. Really.

DETECTIVE Oh, I don't know about that, I wouldn't necessarily say that about you.

JOHN You wouldn't?

DETECTIVE No, I wouldn't, no. You seem special . . . I mean, you said it yourself, that you're some kind of . . . (*Refers to a file.*) You've been "chosen by God." Isn't that right?

JOHN I'm . . . (*Considering.*) I was, yes. Chosen.

DETECTIVE You said it to those first officers. / And you know what's interesting? They don't really wanna talk about it much . . . about when they first found you. Not *one* of 'em wants to. Not on the record. / Why's that?

JOHN That's true . . . / Hmmm. / I have no idea.

DETECTIVE Huh. (*Beat.*) So they went inside and they found you, down on the ground—they said you were, and I'm quoting here, "Subject was completely calm and seemingly in a state of grace." That's a strange way to put it, don't you think? *State of grace.* (*Beat.*) You said that you'd been "spared" by God—I'm assuming that is "God up in heaven?" / That's what you said to them.

JOHN It is. / I did, yes.

DETECTIVE Thirty-seven bodies in that building. I'd say you walk out without a scratch, a man like that is *completely* goddamn special. A bona fide novelty item.

JOHN Right. (*Beat.*) You know what, I'm gonna be honest with you . . .

DETECTIVE I would appreciate that. / It's my job.

JOHN You're making me nervous . . . / Oh. Why? (*Beat.*) What did I do?

DETECTIVE Nothing. (*Laughs.*) Sorry, I don't mean my job is to scare you—I'm saying it's part of the job. *This* job. It unnerves people.

The DETECTIVE *smiles and nods his head. He takes a sip of his own java before thumbing through his file again.*

JOHN You're not . . . I mean, that doesn't mean I'm in trouble. Or anything.

DETECTIVE Not that I'm aware of . . .

JOHN You could just say "no." (*Laughs.*) Right?

DETECTIVE I could. / What?

JOHN That would be a lot more . . . you know . . . / Comforting. For me.

DETECTIVE Yeah, you're probably right. It would be.

JOHN So . . .

DETECTIVE But I don't know that.

JOHN Excuse me? / Oh. That's . . . oh. *What*?

DETECTIVE I'm saying, I do not know for sure that you're not in trouble. / You're not with me, I'm just having you down for a few, you know, follow-up questions. Things that don't seem to add up in the file. A few minor—but otherwise we're good . . . no worries.

JOHN I see. Okay. Wheew! That's . . .

DETECTIVE But I don't know what anybody else down here wants with you, if anything. None of my business . . .

JOHN True. Alright, but with you, it's just . . . what? Some stuff about the . . . tell me.

DETECTIVE Obviously. That day. Questions that still stick out from that day. And since then, but mostly the day of. In question. Even after *60 Minutes*, I still got questions. (*Smiles.*) That Ed Bradley, he seems like an okay guy. Was he?

JOHN   Yes, he was very . . . look, whatever I can be of help with, I'm happy to . . . you can ask me. Anything. / I'm serious, I want to help put all this way behind me and just, you know . . . move on. I do.

DETECTIVE   Great. / That's appreciated. (*Pulls out a pen and makes a notation.*)

JOHN   Did I say something worth . . . ?

DETECTIVE   Just a thought. I'll get back to it.

The DETECTIVE *smiles, then goes back to reading the file.*

JOHN   Don't they usually have cameras in here or something like that? To watch?

DETECTIVE   Occasionally. Not always. / You nervous?

JOHN   Oh. / No. *No*, I just . . . seems like I can't go anywhere these days without being . . .

DETECTIVE   You must see a lotta cop shows. On TV.

JOHN   Yeah. Some.

DETECTIVE   Which do you like?

JOHN   Oh, you know . . . any of the . . .

DETECTIVE   I have no idea. If it's not in your file, it's not something I know. (*Beat.*) Which?

JOHN   Ummmm . . . there's several good . . . *Baretta*, I guess. I used to like that one. Growing up. *Mannix*.

DETECTIVE   Ha! The *realistic* ones, huh?

JOHN   Yep! *Kojak* and all those guys. Classics.

DETECTIVE Right. *Barney Miller.* I like the one guy on that one . . . he was funny.

JOHN Who, Fish?

DETECTIVE Which one was that?

JOHN The old guy. Older. / He was popular.

DETECTIVE No. / Uh-uh, not him. The other one. He had that look on his face . . . / No . . .

JOHN Which one? The balding guy? Polish? / Was it "Wojo?"

DETECTIVE No, the . . . he was Black, maybe. Yeah, he was a colored guy.

JOHN Right. Sure . . . that's Harris. / Ron Glass.

DETECTIVE I dunno. / Maybe.

JOHN That was him. Ron Glass played the part. / He's the actor.

DETECTIVE Yeah? / Could be. He was good on the show, I remember that. (*Does the "look."*) He would do that about anything. He's funny.

JOHN I agree . . .

DETECTIVE So. (*Reading his file.*) How'd you do it?

JOHN Hmmm?

DETECTIVE The picture? Just between you and me?

JOHN I'm not sure what you're . . .

DETECTIVE I know we've gone over this—you said a little something in your first statement and more about it after— the photo. How the hell did you really get that shot? I use *my* camera-phone, pictures are shit and that's me at the *beach*. How the fuck did you take *that*, middle of that mess?

JOHN I just . . . that's . . . ummm . . .

DETECTIVE And why? *Why* would you do it?

JOHN Listen, I feel like you're being kind of confrontational about this, so can we . . . ?

DETECTIVE What?

JOHN I dunno. (*Beat.*) I came down here because I was asked to—I wasn't forced, my own lawyer said I could skip it if I wanted to—and now you're all . . . / You're up in my face with these . . .

DETECTIVE No . . . / I'm not even leaning forward.

JOHN You know what I mean . . .

DETECTIVE No, I'm a very literal person. If you say I'm "up in your face" it would mean more like this . . .

The DETECTIVE *is suddenly out of his seat and right up in* JOHN's *face. Not touching him. Just hovering.*

JOHN . . . ummmm . . .

DETECTIVE Like that. Right-up-in-your-face. That's what it means to me. (*Beat.*) Is that what I was doing? / Was I like that?

JOHN No. / No, you weren't.

DETECTIVE Alright then.

JOHN I meant . . . you know. You know *exactly* what I mean . . . the way your voice was all . . . and insinuating stuff about my . . .

DETECTIVE What? / If you want to. You are free to leave at any time, yes.

JOHN Nothing. Can I go? / But . . . ?

DETECTIVE I'd prefer it if you stayed and answered a few more questions. Put my mind at rest so that I can . . . whatever. Close the book. On you.

JOHN I see.

DETECTIVE Up to you, Mr. Smith.

JOHN Fine. Ask away. If that's how you're . . . I just wish that it didn't have to be so threatening. / Or *imposing*, you know what I'm saying!

DETECTIVE I'm not threatening . . . / All I'm doing is asking a few little . . .

JOHN Come on, be honest! (*Beat.*) You're trying to throw me off here. Make me sweat and I don't even really know . . . what's up?

DETECTIVE Nothing. Honestly.

JOHN I don't believe you.

DETECTIVE I'm sorry.

He smiles and sits back in his chair. JOHN *fidgets a bit.*

JOHN I don't believe that, either.

DETECTIVE Then I'm sorry twice. That's two times in a row now.

JOHN What more could you possibly need to know from me about this thing? Huh?

DETECTIVE I'm just curious—it's not even questions at this point, I'm really just wondering.

JOHN About?

DETECTIVE The picture, like I said. (*Beat.*) Why?

JOHN Because I was . . . as I've said before . . . it felt like someone should *document* what he was doing. / Yes! The horror of it.

DETECTIVE During a shooting? / "Document" while some motherfucker with a machine gun is going around and blowing heads off?

JOHN I wasn't thinking . . . I just . . . I . . .

JOHN *mimes using his camera. The* DETECTIVE *doesn't blink.*

DETECTIVE   "Document." Huh. You decided to just . . . ?

JOHN   Yes. / There wasn't . . . I'm not going to sit here and
defend my . . . what I . . .

DETECTIVE   A guy who could've got outta there, saved his own
skin or maybe . . . just *maybe* helped somebody else out
through the back door or whatever. Why didn't you do that? /
If you're such a big Christian now—got God there telling you
what to do—how come he didn't direct you to save a few of
those people who were getting shot in the face instead of
snapping a photo? Hmm? Why do you think that is? A picture
that you've now made a pretty good profit off of . . . made you
famous . . . / You *know* they have.

JOHN   I kept very little of the . . . / Look, *most* funds from the
picture sale were donated out to various charities and, and,
and . . .

JOHN *finally stops trying to explain, throwing his hands up in*
frustration. Silence. DETECTIVE *stays seated.*

DETECTIVE   I'm just asking . . . (*Beat.*) In my job, you find that
sort of thing interesting. Why people act one way. Or the
other.

JOHN   I didn't run off . . . I mean, I didn't just take off down the
stairs and save my skin or anything, so . . . I'm . . .

DETECTIVE   Very true. I've corroborated that.

JOHN   Yes, so I didn't just . . . people need to be aware of that.
What *really* happened.

DETECTIVE   I'm sure we'll be putting out a statement that

supports all this, as well . . . they're also working on a documentary, CNN or one of those stations, so . . . / It'll happen.

JOHN   Then good. / Fine. Because . . . I just . . .

DETECTIVE   Which brings us full circle. / To you.

JOHN   . . . and? / I don't understand.

DETECTIVE   Nothing. Just "why." I'm gonna leave you with that. (*Beat.*) As a cop and a man of a certain age and a Christian—I'm actually one of only a few people in this town who don't mind saying that they love the Lord and have Christian beliefs and values—as all of those things I find your story to be completely full of shit. Sorry. / And I want it to be true! I do! I touch you or put a hand on your shoulder . . . like this . . .

The DETECTIVE *touches* JOHN *on the arm. Holds his tight.*

DETECTIVE   Nothing. I don't feel a thing. And I even met Billy Graham when I was younger so I do know what goodness is all about, I do—and I'm telling you right now, if I felt that from you I'd drop what I was doing, throw my fucking badge on the table this instant and follow you right outta this room. Promise you I would . . . (*Beat.*) But I don't get any of that from you. Not one drop. (*Beat.*) Now I wonder why that is . . .

JOHN   What? / Why're you . . . *what*? I mean . . .

DETECTIVE   Hey . . . It's just an observation.

JOHN   Yeah, but . . . why would even . . . ?

DETECTIVE   It's not libel because I'm not talking to Larry King, so don't worry . . .

JOHN   Still, you can't . . . that's not very . . .

DETECTIVE I can say whatever the hell I want to. To you. Here. In private. / I just did.

JOHN But you're . . . / I did nothing wrong!

DETECTIVE You *survived*. That's always suspect, my friend. Didn't you know that?

JOHN . . . but I'm . . . listen, I was . . .

DETECTIVE You lived. You took a photo. You made a fortune off it, whether you kept it or not.

JOHN What was I supposed to do? Huh?!

DETECTIVE Something. Anything other than take that *picture* of the guy, with your coworkers dying. *Any*thing but that . . . (*Beat.*) And when they do find you, finally get there to where you are—you're all blissed out like nothing ever happened. Acting all . . .

JOHN . . . yes? So?

DETECTIVE I mean, if you had *really* been converted that day . . . / Seems to me that if God had *really* taken the time to come down and to choose somebody, pick out some guy to . . .

JOHN What? / *What*? Go on, say it.

DETECTIVE I, for one, don't think we'd be sitting here talking today.

JOHN No? / Well, I'm . . . that's not my . . .

DETECTIVE No way. / Not at all.

JOHN Why? I mean . . .

DETECTIVE Because you would've done something dumb! Folks who think they have God inside do the stupidest shit on earth. They attack the enemy in their *underwear*, they stop a bank robber with their *purse*, grandmas lift *Cadillacs* up and off of babies . . . crap like that. So. (*Beat.*) You would've confronted this guy, you would've tried to talk him down and you would've gotten shot in the chest for your troubles . . . You'd be dead now. *If* God was actually with you that day.

JOHN   That's not true. You don't know . . .

DETECTIVE   I know enough. I've seen so much shit in my lifetime as a cop that I can guess how a person is going to act or what they'll say or figure out what the heart of the matter is *ninety-nine* times outta one hundred. Seriously. That many times. (*Beat.*) And your story . . . it stinks.

JOHN   Don't say that.

DETECTIVE   . . . I already did. You lived, that's *your* problem. You get to go around and talk to Leno and sell your photo . . . but you know the truth . . . inside you *know.* Somehow this is all connected and you're not . . . / You are not being honest with me. You're not!

JOHN   I'm . . . / Look, I'm going . . .

JOHN *gets to his feet. The* DETECTIVE *sits and watches him go.* JOHN *turns back to him abruptly and speaks.*

JOHN   God came to me . . . he came and told me to wait. He *commanded* me to, to, to stay in there . . . / Stop saying that!! God came to me . . . he came and he *lifted* me up . . .

DETECTIVE   No, he didn't. / You're a liar.

JOHN   I'm not! No, I'm not!! I'm leaving now . . .

DETECTIVE   Run. / Run if you wanna but you're lying. You are *holding* something back!

JOHN   Stop it!! / Stop saying that!!!

DETECTIVE   You are lying to yourself and everybody you know.

JOHN   . . . this is ridiculous . . . you can't . . .

JOHN *turns and heads toward the door again. The* DETECTIVE *calls out again. Holds up his notepad.*

DETECTIVE   Wait! Mr. Smith. One question. Let me ask another question and I will never bother you again, not ever. / Promise.

JOHN   Yeah? / Really?

DETECTIVE   I said "promise."

JOHN   Go ahead then . . . (*Waits.*) Go on.

DETECTIVE   Was there any reason that you can think of, any at all, that our shooter would single you out *not* to kill?/ Mr. Diaz, who sat very near you day in and out for however long— why would he let you go?

JOHN   *What?* / I have no . . . I mean, why're . . . ?

DETECTIVE   He seemed to have a grudge against one of your bosses at least and pretty much the whole place—he had a lotta *wrath* in 'em, obviously, and hell, you're the guy who let 'em go! *Fired* his ass—so is there a reason that if he was in there, *blasting* away at people and he comes upon you . . . that he wouldn't kill you? (*Beat.*) Anything? You gave him lunch money one day or, I dunno, smiled at him once? Whatever. I always wanted to ask you that . . .

JOHN   This is . . . that's . . . what're you implying?

DETECTIVE   Nothing, I'm just asking.

JOHN   I'm . . . no . . . I have to leave . . .

DETECTIVE   It's just a question. / Just answer the . . .

JOHN   I'm going . . . / No! I'm leaving now.

DETECTIVE   Tell me the *truth!*

JOHN   I have! I told you the truth and now I'm leaving!

DETECTIVE Why won't those cops talk about what they saw in there? Tell me that, Mr. Smith?! *What* did they see?!?

JOHN *goes to the door and pulls the handle. Won't budge at all. He tries again, each time getting more desperate.*

JOHN It's . . . / It isn't working. / It's stuck!
DETECTIVE . . . you have to push to get out. / (*Mimes a pushing motion.*) No, just give it a little bit of . . . / You have to . . . that's it. Push.

JOHN *keeps trying it—the door finally swings open.* JOHN *slips through and disappears down the hall.*

After a moment, the DETECTIVE *gestures toward the mirror. Makes a cutting motion across his throat. Sits back.*

A burst of intense light carries us on to:

A perfect circle of stained glass overhead. Dominating everything else. JOHN, *in a suit, stands looking at us.*

JOHN   This is what is left, my brothers and sisters. For me to cleanse myself. Just the truth now. Thank you for joining me at this service today as I need to tell you all this, and then you can do with it whatever you will. I can live with that, because this is necessary, doing this has been on my mind for some time and I need to get it out in the open. Unload myself of it. Is that alright? (*Beat.*) I hope so, because—wiser minds than my own say it's so. (*Beat.*) You are my flock and you grow day by day—others do not hear, or hear and hate what they hear. But not you. You've stood next to me as I've slowly made my way into the divine light of His glory. Others scoffed when they heard my past—infidelities and the rest—as I have slowly washed myself clean. And yet more remains. If you leave me now I will both understand and forgive you—but if I am to do what God wants of me, what I have been *singled* out to do . . . then you must first know the complete truth. Hear me now.

JOHN *moves about, talking to the congregation in front of him. His confidence growing.*

JOHN   I never wanted this—I'm like most every other person out there . . . meaning I just wanted to finish working with a bit of money in my pocket and retire to Florida or, or, I dunno, *Arizona* and hang out in a bar with friends and that'd be it. I'm not a guy who wants to be senator, to be an elected official or noticed when he's walking down the street. I've got as much ego as the next person but not to where I have some inflated sense of worth. Nobody knows more than me what it's like to be a regular person and I'm good with that. No need for any fanfare here. (*Beat.*) This is the work of some*thing*—if you don't like saying "God" then call it whatever else you wanna say, but he spared me on that day. He did, and you can laugh at me or giggle as you recount the story to your friends, but I know what happened there. It wasn't luck. It wasn't skill or the *cavalry* charging over the hilltops one morning—and it won't make me live any longer or give me special powers. Nothing like that. If anything, my life is worse now because I'm *aware*. I know what I'm set apart to do, how I am supposed to live. I have to be kind every day, try and set an example for the world and hope that others will follow me, even change their ways. (*Beat.*) They might not. I just might turn you *into a smoker* for all I know, just 'cause you dislike me so damn much once you hear my story . . . well okay. That's on you. But that's what I get for surviving, for coming out of there alive. I need to try and set an example while I go about living my life. I can't deny it and I can't escape it. *This* is who I am now. I'm John Smith and I'm not—I am a child of God and one of those Christian soldiers you hear about, in that one song . . . marching as to . . . yes.

He waits a moment, considering what to say. Starts once and stops. Begins again.

JOHN   It wasn't always so. I have been cleansed by the love of my Father in Heaven and in the blood of his son, Jesus Christ, but I harbor a dark and horrible fear. It isn't a sin nor something any priest or pastor can ever lift from my shoulders . . . (*Beat.*) Juan Diaz was well known to me. He wasn't good at his job—that hardly matters now but it's true and may be of note to this somehow in the end—he was a useless part of the Sanford-Gross team and we all knew it. He was protected under some branch of affirmative action and no doubt some man or woman of a whiter shade of skin lost out on the job due to filling a quota in our company by hiring him. No doubt about that at all. He barely spoke English, had terrible phone skills, and was constantly asking—if not me then my assistant or those around me—for help with our filing system, computer issues, the works. The man was out of his league and he knew it. He could not keep up! The fact that this hasn't come up in any of the published stories about the incident surprises me, but I've kept quiet about it for obvious reasons, as you will see . . .

JOHN *shifts his weight now. Clears his throat. Starts in once again on his story.*

JOHN　. . . Mr. Diaz—"Juan," was his given name, it was "Juan"—was not a friendly man or a guy who you could, you know, you wouldn't warm to him, nobody did, over the time he was in our office. He was an outsider and I suppose a few of us—me maybe even more than the rest—eventually started making sure that he remained that way. It wasn't anything that most people would notice . . . that's probably why nobody has said anything—my colleagues went unaware of what a few of us were doing to him over the course of six or seven months . . . (*Beat.*) When a detective asked me once if I could think of why he might've let me live I almost laughed . . .

really, almost in his face because that's such an absurd idea! If anything, it was the exact opposite. Mr. Diaz probably, no I'm *certain* of it, he no doubt hated me—

my coworkers and me—more than anybody on the face of the earth. I cannot say that things we did caused him to go over the edge because I'm not sure . . . wasn't mentioned in his e-mails, which surprised the hell out of me! I was relieved, too, obviously . . . but that was unexpected. And no one else knew . . . or they died on that day. Carried it to their graves and I was the only one left who knows what happened. Or, why it happened, I guess. "Why." (*Beat.*) We would call his phone. Buzz it constantly from various rooms in the building, send him on errands to meet employees down in the lobby who didn't exist and would not be waiting. He was a fairly religious person, I believe, from what I've been told, and we would send him porn to his computer . . . the nastiest sort of girls-with-animals-or-licking-cream-out-of-some-man's-ass-porn we could find. It was *so* filthy! God help us, I'm a man in my forties and I was . . . well, I was acting like a child! (*Beat.*) A friend of mine . . . a salesman who was shot that day—he did this, like, massive poop in his desk one time. Over lunch. I mean, he did it out in the bathroom but carried it in on a paper towel and laid it out in the lower drawer. Unbelievable . . . (*Waits.*) That made him cry, actually, now that I think about it. Juan sat at his desk and wept when he found that. He sat looking around the room with these short little turns of his head . . . not knowing why or who or what for. But that's the sort of thing we did. (*Beat.*) And then he was let go. He was given two weeks' notice but he never came back to us once he got that letter handed to him. I did it, I mean, put it in his hands—as the Operations Manager, that was my job. I gave him a little smile and a wink, even— I was a complete and full-time asshole in those days, I admit it—I handed it to him and off I trotted, back over to my friends and laughing. And Juan never showed up during those two weeks at all. It was almost a month before he came into the, well . . . you're aware of what he did.

JOHN *stops, takes a couple of deep breaths, looking hard into the light. He continues.*

JOHN That moment . . . when he was standing over me—I've gone on record as saying that I don't know what happened. That there were lights and noise and God came to me . . . all that is true. It is. But I did see more. More than I've let on, until now. (*Beat.*) He's now standing over me—Mr. Diaz—with this gun in my face and a look . . . I don't feel like I've ever seen a face like that on a living person. He wasn't there, I mean . . . obviously he was, he was doing all this but he was in some other place. Talking in, in, like, Spanish but babbling—I'm able to speak a little and it wasn't any that I'd ever heard—with his eyes almost completely rolled back, just the edges of his pupils were visible but he's looking down at me. Smiling. Licking his lips and this gun pointed in my face. He put this huge . . . gun . . . its *barrel* . . . into my mouth and he pulled the trigger. And nothing. And again. Nothing. Click. Click. Click. Without looking away he discharged the clip and slammed in another. As it went in I could see the bullets spilling out the top of it—completely full. He made me take it back into my . . . (*he wavers*) . . . this is very hard for me to . . . I had to put it back into my throat and then he did it again. Pulled the trigger . . . click. Oh Christ, I was . . . I dunno, this couldn't be happening! There I was, on my knees with a machine gun in my face and he's . . . it's impossible to explain. You try it. I don't know how. (*Beat.*) A second later there's the sound of police in the hall, the screams of people dying and Juan looks at me. He looks at me and do you know what he did? He turned the gun on himself. He shrugged like, you know, like I'd asked him a science question that he couldn't figure out—he *shrugged* and put the gun in his own mouth. Pulled the trigger once and it roared. BAM! This spray of blood went, oh-my-God, it was . . . everywhere . . . and he dropped to the ground. At my feet. The police came past us, on the run down the hall seconds later and there was the light pouring in now, the noise of all the . . . but I was completely lucid at that moment, just before . . . and I promise you this: what I've just told you is the absolute and God's-honest truth . . . I have no reason to lie now, or hold back on the facts. It's been eating me alive . . . all that I still knew about it, but I didn't think the world would be . . . ready. That I had the *right* to say all this. To offer up this gospel *truth*. Until now.

JOHN *leans forward now—intent on telling the rest of his story.*

JOHN I was not a good person. In my life. That must be obvious to you by now. There was no reason for God to single me out, use a man like me for any reason other than it being a part of his almighty and infinite plan. Why else? Hmmm?

(*Beat.*) I can't go and change the world—I can barely make anybody believe what's happened to me! But I *must*—I have to soldier on now to let others know my story, and I think I now understand the reason. Why I'm here. Because I'm not a doubter. No matter who I was and what . . . *ill* . . . I did before with my life, now is different. I'm filled to the top with a spirit that can't be left out or pushed aside—I know what God is expecting of me. Do all the wrongs I've made get washed away with each hand that I shake, every time someone smiles over at me and whispers, "I believe you, John"? I dunno. I'm not sure. Will the thirty-seven dead ever be worth the lives I'll change or any good I might do? Impossible to say. But I do know that a life half-lived is better than one not lived at all and what used to be my unrepentant heart is now awash in the love of Christ!

JOHN *gets down on his knees. Motions toward the heavens.*

JOHN I was lost but now I'm found. I despair over the human cost but know it is not mine to consider. (*Beat.*) I am only a man and time will answer my questions: My wife will return to me or not. The world will accept my calling or they won't. No more sadness will come from my adultery or there will be a hell for both of us to pay—I can't know the future and do not wish to. But I accept it! I do not and never will again fight the feeling of righteousness in my heart. This spark of light I feel right here . . . (*Pointing.*) We all have it, every one of us. We know when something sits correctly with us or not, secretly we do, but we try to shake it off, say it's just us being weak or superstitious or whatever works in the moment. Chest pains! (*Beat.*) But we know. We *know* . . . we all know on the inside. We do. I know we do. I *know* it!

JOHN'*s eyes close as his head falls back. He is talking feverishly now, caught up in the moment.*

JOHN   If you could . . . I so wish that any of you might've shared that moment with me! That day, as I knelt there, a dead man at my feet and not understanding, not able to comprehend the magnitude of . . . with this light, a kind of heavenly light spilling in and, yes, I'm aware of police and all the people running, the tear gas clouds swirling around, but I was steadfast . . . the voice of God was there and I could hear the . . . sound of angels from above. And for a moment—the briefest of tiny moments in my lifetime—I was free. No past to regret and no future of worries. Just the moment, hovering there, filled with tears and love and golden blessings. And I began to fill up . . . to be filled up with the goodness of a thousand tomorrows and, my God, I was floating . . . there I was in my suit and my tie but I was *floating* above it all . . . just . . .

*And for a moment it's true—*JOHN SMITH *rises slightly off the ground. Eyes closed, hands and head turned up. Smile spread wide across his face. An ethereal music begins to build.*

JOHN   For a single moment the sun broke through the clouds at noon and I was one with all goodness that had ever come before me and all that would ever grace mankind again—

and it was peaceful and I was filled with hope and bliss and promise. Oh God, oh my sweet, sweet Lord on high! Such glory and such promise!

JOHN SMITH *is hovering there, somewhere between heaven and earth. Lost in a moment of complete and utter reverie.*

A burst of intense light surrounds him. Swallows him up. He is gone as we too must avert our gaze from the stage. The brightness is simply too overpowering.

Silence. Darkness.